The Other Side of Dailiness

"The Other Side of Dailiness":

Photography in the Works of Alice Munro, Timothy Findley, Michael Ondaatje, and Margaret Laurence

✛

Lorraine M. York

✛

ECW PRESS

+

CANADIAN CATALOGUING IN PUBLICATION DATA

York, Lorraine Mary, 1958–
The other side of dailiness

Bibliography: p.
Includes index.
ISBN 1-55022-003-9 (bound). – ISBN 1-55022-002-0 (pbk.).

1. Canadian literature (English) – 20th century –
History and criticism.* 2. Literature and photography – Canada.
I. Title.

PS8191.P43Y67 1988 C813'.54'09 C87-093316-7
PR9192.6.P43Y67 1988

The Other Side of Dailiness has been published
with the assistance of a grant from the
Canadian Federation for the Humanities,
using funds provided by the
Social Sciences and Humanities Research Council of Canada.
Additional grants have been provided by
The Canada Council and the Ontario Arts Council.

Cover design and artwork by The Dragon's Eye Press, Toronto.
Typeset by ECW Production Services, Oakville.
Printed and bound by the University of Toronto Press, Downsview.
Published by ECW PRESS, 307 Coxwell Avenue, Toronto, Ont. M4L 3B5

+

+ TABLE OF CONTENTS +

✦ ACKNOWLEDGEMENTS ✦

A number of people read this work in its early stages and gave me valuable advice about its publication: John Ferns, Carl Ballstadt, Linda Hutcheon, Joan Coldwell, Magdalene Redekop, Louis Greenspan, Paul Walton, Robert Lecker, and Francesca Worrall; and readers for the Canadian Federation for the Humanities.

I owe as well special thanks to Reginald and Margaret York for kindnesses too numerous to count, to Gillian Middleton for friendship, and to Michael Ross for sharing so cheerfully my photographic obsessions.

No one escapes the perjury of time;
This permanence that light and shade have struck
So brave in attitude, I would believe
Essential and innocent of change.

– Howard Nemerov, "An Old Photograph"

Introduction

+

" A Message with a Code "

The early twentieth-century photographer and sociologist Lewis Hine once remarked: "If I could tell the story in words, I wouldn't need to lug a camera" (qtd. in Gutman 19). Photography is, as Hine sensed, a form of narrative, and it has recently been the task of theorists both in literature and the visual arts to investigate this relationship more systematically than ever before. Indeed, theorists dealing with philosophical issues such as knowledge and perception have repeatedly been drawn to the photographic image, as if to some central and mysterious icon which will, under careful scrutiny, divulge its secrets. In particular, the photograph has been the starting point for many thinkers to query the concept of objectivity, or, to use E.H. Gombrich's term, the "innocent eye." The reason for the photograph's privileged position in these discussions is its dual relation to the world. On the one hand there is the common assumption that a photograph reproduces the world, an assumption which is difficult to break. On the other hand there is ample evidence that the photograph "lies," that it transforms, rather than represents, reality.

This dual status of photography makes it an ideal vehicle for examining the assumptions about perception and knowledge which one finds in literary texts. In the works of twentieth-century modernists and postmodernists – the first two generations to use photography in a thorough-going way – one finds not only photographic metaphors but photographically

9

inspired literary structures. In an intellectual era which has witnessed intense inquiry into the concepts of reality and of literature, it is not surprising that many literary texts are, through the agency of the photograph, asking some of the same questions.

Roland Barthes was among the first to place the photograph at the centre of the twentieth-century debate over perception and reality. In a much-celebrated phrase from *Image Music Text* he described the photograph as "a message without a code." "Certainly," he wrote, "the image is not the reality but at least it is its perfect *analogon* . . . " (17). Barthes was, however, careful to point out that the photographic message is more complex than his formulation might suggest; it is, in fact, paradoxical, since it consists of both an uncoded denotative message and a coded connotative one. Nevertheless, the denotative function is, for Barthes, axiomatic – "the connoted (or coded) message develops on the basis of a message *without a code*" (19) – a formulation which is nothing if not paradoxical. This privileging of the denotative message of the photographic image reaches its height in Barthes's claim that "the denoted image [of the photograph] can appear as a kind of Edenic state of the image . . . " (42).

If poststructuralist theory has taught critics of literature and the visual arts anything, it has taught them to mistrust the positing of any phenomenon as "Edenic," or captured forever in a perfect, pristine state. For this reason, more recent photography theorists have disagreed profoundly with Barthes's location of the denotative photographic message in a never-never land, removed from human culture. Umberto Eco, by 1970, could write: "[t]he theory of the photo as an *analogue* has been abandoned, even by those who once upheld it . . . . We know that the image which takes shape on celluloid is analogous to the retinal image but not to that which we perceive" (33). Victor Burgin admits that "the [photographic] image is in a sense *caused* by its referent," since the emulsion does react to the amount of light present, but that does not alter, for him, the fact that "[t]he photograph abstracts from, and mediates, the actual" (61). Thus Barthes's distinction between drawing ("which even when denoted, is a coded message" [19]) and photography ("a message without a code") collapses.

These theorists were so eager to correct Barthes's view

(even though he had allowed the photograph both denotative and connotative meaning, both nature and culture) because they were engaged in a fight against earlier realist conceptions of photography. The nineteenth-century view of photography as a "window on the world" still persists in the twentieth century, as any glance at photographic criticism will prove. Like their colleagues in literary theory, visual theorists were striving in the 1970s to focus critical attention away from what the art object contained or represented, towards its constitutive processes, the processes of making meaning. In order to do this, they adopted several strategies (all of which find their equivalents in recent literary theory), such as unmasking the subjectivity of the photograph, undermining conventional notions of photographic truth, and reevaluating the role of culture in a medium traditionally associated with nature.

Establishing the subjectivity of photography is not a difficult matter; here the theorist is able to place the findings of the physical sciences against commonplace assumptions. Physiological studies have shown that we do not see the images on our retinas; we edit and transform those images so that they conform to our expectations regarding relative size, perspective, and so on. Furthermore, we do not see all the objects in our visual field with the clarity of detail one sees in photographs; a photograph of a cathedral nave will preserve many more details of the apse area than a person with good eyesight will be able to see at any one moment. Conversely, there are experiential elements of vision which the photographic image does not necessarily transmit. E.H. Gombrich uses four photographs of a statue of Stephenson, the inventor of the railway engine, to illustrate this point. What appears in one photograph to be a building far behind the bronze figure is unmasked in another as an air vent which is quite close to the statue. A shot taken with a wide-angle lens presents an entirely different spatial relationship between the two objects. The addition of human figures at certain places in some of the photographs similarly plays havoc with our notions of scale and distance (Gombrich 185-87). As Gombrich concludes, "The image cannot give us more information than the medium can carry" (192).

Closely allied to this attack on photographic objectivity is the contemporary attack on the notion of truth as applied to photographic images. Deconstruction, with its theory of the constant deferral of meaning, has influenced photographic, perceptual, and literary theories alike. Truth, as a stable concept, becomes problematic in relation to photography; Gombrich uses the example of two x-rays, one which appears to be clearer, more sharply defined, and one which appears fuzzier, with fewer details and contrasts. The seemingly clear image, however, conceals a pathological condition which is only visible in the "fuzzier" x-ray (183-84). He supplies a theory of truth for the visual image which recalls his concept of schema and correction in *Art and Illusion*; that is, we adapt ourselves to what the photograph shows (blurry images of figures in motion, for instance) and we label such phenomena "true," even though we do not perceive them in this way. What we are left with is no longer the nineteenth-century conception of photographic truth, that of the window on the world, but various humanly constructed notions of visual truth.

What theorists such as Gombrich show us is the role of human culture in a supposedly natural visual object. Indeed, the conflict between nature and culture has been a key part of recent debates in photographic theory. To a great extent, this debate was incited by Barthes, who asked in *Image Music Text*: "how then can the photograph be at once 'objective' and 'invested,' natural and cultural?" (20). "One day," he predicted, it may "be possible to reply to that question" (20). Recent theorists, especially those interested in cultural concerns, have seized upon Barthes's invitation. Frank Webster, writing about what can in 1980 be called "the new photography," answers Barthes's question – appropriately – with a paradox of his own. The photographic image, he argues, "both requires a cultural milieu in which its symbols can be comprehensibly interpreted ... while simultaneously staying aloof from a context which facilitates the cognition of an image's meaning. Photography both needs culture for effective communication and remains autonomous from culture" (153). But, one must ask, can such a paradoxical formulation remain as it is, suspended and held together through the tension of apparent opposites? For once one admits that the photograph needs culture, can one sustain the other half of the paradox – its aesthetic autonomy? Several theorists would answer with a resounding "no," and they have chosen to concentrate on the photograph as a partaker in a system of signification which is, like all other such systems, necessarily rooted in culture. One thinks, for instance, of John Berger, whose studies of visual images in *Ways of Seeing* (1972) and *Another Way of Telling* (1982) always emphasize the importance of cultural meanings in the decoding of visual signs. In fact, photographic theorists have allied themselves so closely to the cultural side of the nature–culture debate that Joel Snyder could write in 1980 that once theorists have tired of their discussions of "the ontological status of photographs," they will move to a more searching question: "How is it that we ever came to think of photographs as being natural phenomena at all?" (234).

The history of photography – or, more precisely, the history of the perception of photography – supplies part of the answer to Snyder's question. The earliest creators and users of photography justified the new invention by this very recourse to the natural; Daguerre called it "a chemical and physical process which gives Nature the ability to reproduce herself" (qtd. in Newhall, *The History of Photography* 17), Oliver Wendell Holmes christened the photograph "the mirror with a memory" (qtd. in Newhall 22), and William Henry Fox Talbot's 1844 collection of calotypes (an early photographic variant and his own invention) appeared under the title *The Pencil of Nature.* Why were these early pioneers of photography so eager to see the new invention as the product of a personified nature? If one looks at the historical context, the answer becomes clear. The *camera obscura* and *camera lucida*, the apparatus which preceded the cameras of Daguerre and Talbot, still involved the complicity of a human hand; as the box-like tool threw the outlines of the natural scene upon the paper, the artist faithfully traced them. Thus the notion of the landscape imprinting itself on the empty copper plate, without the agency of the human hand (save the chemical operations performed prior to and after the exposure) was utterly unheard of. That the cult of nature as artist should have arisen in photographic discourse is hardly surprising.

In succeeding decades, as the photographic methods became less cumbersome and time-consuming, human beings could come to feel that they had gained some mastery over a process which had initially seemed nothing short of a miracle.

Dry plates, rapid shutter speeds, even colour – all were instances of the human being behind the lens grasping the pencil of nature. As a result, nature and culture have been diametrically opposed elements since the beginning; the history of photography is, like the history of the steam engine or the automobile, a story of culture's continual struggle for ascendancy over nature.

If one surveys the movements in photography from the mid-nineteenth to the mid-twentieth centuries, one sees a dialectical struggle between culture and nature. The pioneering emphasis on the pencil of nature soon gave way in the 1850s and 1860s to a desire for pictorial effect; photographers aped painting, masked and combined negatives to achieve aesthetic effects. In the 1870s and 1880s, the pendulum swung back; the photographs of Eakins and Muybridge documented movement – humans walking, horses galloping. The revolution in theories of perception which these documents incited is aptly illustrated by a well-known example. Eadweard Muybridge's serial photographs of a horse galloping showed that the horse did indeed lift all four feet from the ground at one point, but the legs were not, as was formerly thought and depicted in the visual arts, outstretched, but tucked in towards the body. Culture had entirely transformed human beings' conceptions of nature, of visual truth. In the closing years of the nineteenth century and the first decades of the twentieth, photographers such as Alfred Stieglitz, Edward Steichen, and Clarence White returned to an aestheticist conception of photography. The group to which they belonged, "Photo Secession" or "291" (their gallery was located at 291 Fifth Avenue), sought to establish photography as a fine art. These photographic modernists were interested in the interplay of forms, light, and shadow in their photographs, and although they did not engage in the allegorical photography of their nineteenth-century pictorialist predecessors, they believed that, in Stieglitz's words, "[i]t is justifiable to use any means upon a negative or paper to attain the desired end" (qtd. in Newhall 105). But the nature–culture balance was about to tip decisively towards nature in the 1920s and 1930s, with the advent of straight and documentary photography. The former, as practised by Paul Strand, Edward Weston, and Ansel Adams, was vehemently opposed to pictorialism and manipulation. Weston's extremely detailed photographs of Californian sand dunes – every ripple and edge rendered crisply and sharply – are perfect examples of this approach. In fact, both he and Adams became members of the "Group f.64," named for the small apertures which these photographers used in order to capture the minutest detail. The documentary photographers such as Lewis Hine, Jacob Riis, and Walker Evans turned this emphasis on natural detail to political ends; the first two photographing with uncompromising honesty the urban poor, and Evans, most memorably in *Let Us Now Praise Famous Men*, the rural poor.

But aestheticism was not so easily overturned, and to this day the nature-culture split persists in photographic theory. While Strand and Evans were photographing rickety white fences and frame houses, experimenters such as Man Ray and Lazlo Moholy-Nagy were exploring the aesthetic effects of multiple exposures and photographic collage. Both trends – realism and abstraction – can be found in the exhibitions and catalogues of contemporary photographers. The nature-culture dialectic has, in fact, so characterized photography from its inception that one could imagine writing a history of photography based on Gombrich's theory of Western art, with its alternating trends towards abstraction or stylization and representation.

In current photographic theory culture is dominant. Joel Snyder's theorist is poised to ask his/her question: how could we ever have conceived of the photograph as natural? One result of the current theoretical ascendancy of culture has been the politicization of photographic theory. For Barthes, denotation is foremost in the photograph, and is "powerless to alter political opinions: no photograph has ever convinced or refuted anyone . . . " (30). As contemporary theorists have shown, however, photography – whether denotative or connotative – is political. The denotative effect of concentration camp photographs is, as we shall see in Timothy Findley's *Famous Last Words*, a power to be reckoned with. Furthermore, critics like John Berger, Frank Webster, Victor Burgin, and even Barthes himself, have decoded individual photographic systems and unmasked their political connotations.

War photographs are among the most overtly political, and since they play a major role in chapter 2, they deserve some preliminary theoretical consideration here. Photographs of wartime action invoke nature and denotation – how could a photographer arrange the heated events of a battlefield? – but this semblance of objectivity masks a powerful connotative element. Indeed, the war photograph makes the nature-culture distinction an ethical problem. George Rodger, for instance, was probably the first to photograph Belsen in 1945. Instinctively, he began to take photographs of the horrific scene before him when suddenly he realized that he was framing the dead bodies in front of him in aesthetically pleasing patterns. He resolved on the spot never again to photograph war (Lewinski 14). This anecdote dramatizes the way in which the nature-culture dichotomy which is basic to photography becomes, ultimately, a political dichotomy. To photograph war is, by definition, to photograph human misery, and the act of photographing places the photographer, try though he or she might to convey sympathy for the victims, in the position of intruder and exploiter. This uneasy position is summed up in two Vietnam war photographers' experiments with a camera which could be fastened to a gun, enabling the photographer-killer to capture on film the moment of death (Lewinski 17). This interplay between camera and gun becomes a favourite image of highly politicized contemporary writers like Timothy Findley and Michael Ondaatje, who begin to suspect that the pen is equally indicted along with the gun and camera in the war to capture and transfix nature.

This association opens up one of the most fascinating debates in recent photographic theory; the relationship between photography and language. If photography is imbued with culture, then it must be "a message with a code" (to alter Barthes's phrase), a language. Semiotic theories applied to photography have opened up the possibility that photography, like language, is a signifying system. Originally, theorists like Barthes studied the literal relationship between photography and language – the coproduction of meaning through photographs and captions. In the press photograph, at least, Barthes found the role of accompanying text to be "repressive"; it fixes or "anchors" meaning (40) – a power relationship explored by postmodernist writers such as Ondaatje who reproduce actual photographs in their texts.

Other theorists have followed in Barthes's footsteps, emphasizing the word's power to fix the image, to impose meaning on it. "Because photographs are open to a variety of interpretations," writes Frank Webster, "they have a desperate need for words which can fix a particular interpretation" (162), or, as Susan Sontag asserts: "[O]nly that which narrates can make us understand" (*On Photography* 23). Both statements underline the power which these two theorists have invested in the word ("desperate need," "*make* us understand" [emphasis added]). Poststructuralist critics would see no need for the bullying word, nor would they insist on the need for a single conception of "interpretation." Because they see photography as language, the power struggle dissolves; the viewer is not forced to understand, but free to create for himself or herself a variety of readings of the visual image. "[P]hotographs are *texts* inscribed in terms of what we may call 'photographic discourse,'" writes Victor Burgin, "but this discourse, like any other, engages discourses beyond itself . . . previous texts 'taken for granted' at a particular cultural and historical juncture" (144). The recognition of photography as a language system and the politicization of photography thus go hand in hand.

Of particular interest to a study such as this one are the links between photography and narrative. Of course, photographs have been used to ape narrative, not only in the nineteenth-century pictorialists' experiments but more recently in the "photo-story" made popular by publications such as *Life*. But the very fact that one feels tempted to place photographs in a certain sequence in order to reproduce a linear narrative (such as in Margaret Laurence's *The Diviners*) should tell us that the narrative qualities of the single photograph are *not* linear. Rather, narrative in photographs is always implied narrative – the freezing of a moment in time, because it excludes the moments before and after the exposure, irresistibly impresses upon us the linearity of experienced time and our own inability to freeze time. As a result, many contemporary writers who are themselves faced with the traditional conceptions of plot and narrative, and who are experimenting with fictional forms which emphasize non-linearity, find in photography a ready analogue.

This alliance between writers and photography is, as I have mentioned, most pronounced in modernist and postmodernist writers, including many Canadian writers. If I had wanted to write an exhaustive survey of Canadian writers who use photographic metaphors and structures in their works, I would have faced a preliminary list containing at least the following names: Alice Munro, Timothy Findley, Michael Ondaatje, Margaret Laurence, Al Purdy, Brian Moore, Margaret Atwood, Guy Vanderhaeghe, Leonard Cohen, Marian Engel, Roch Carrier, Rudy Wiebe, Joy Kogawa, Jack Hodgins, Heather Robertson, Audrey Thomas, Robert Kroetsch, and Hugh Hood. Instead, I have chosen to focus on the first four writers listed above, for several interconnected reasons. First of all, a closer focus allows me to study the evolution of a particular writer's relationship to the photographic image, and in most cases I find the evolution of that relationship to be extremely pronounced. More important, though, is the relationship between the type of fiction a writer is creating and his or her attitude towards photography. Is a postmodernist writer's obsession with the camera qualitatively different from that of a traditional realist? Quite early in my chapter on Alice Munro I refer to George Bowering's labelling of Munro as a traditional realist (a view with which I differ). In the same article, entitled "Modernism Could Not Last Forever," Bowering argues that postmodernism is a photographically conscious movement whereas traditional mimetic realism is not. In a sense, this study is a qualification of that distinction.

Alice Munro and Timothy Findley, Michael Ondaatje and Margaret Laurence: I chose these four Canadian writers because they are ideal subjects for my study. The group comprises two postmodernists: Findley and Ondaatje; one traditional realist: Laurence; and Munro, whose works straddle the boundary between realism and postmodernism. Both realists and postmodernists may be conscious of photography, but it is the *nature* of their consciousness and their engagement with photography which distinguishes them from each other, since photography, as we have seen, simply provides another way of thinking about perception and reality.

This dual emphasis on form and photographic consciousness has also influenced the structure of this study. The chapters, instead of following a chronological order, reflect my interest in fictional approach. I place Alice Munro first because her perception of photography unmasks its paradoxical nature, and the terms involved in these paradoxes provide necessary background for my study of the other three writers. One sees in Munro's work the tensions, the contrasting sets of conditions associated with the photographic image. Because of the paradoxical nature of Munro's vision I have also decided not to structure the chapter dealing with her fiction in a chronological, developmental fashion. Paradox is the holding of opposites in balance and such a view militates against any sense of evolution in Munro's perception of photography. She has said that she does not see human destiny in terms of continual progression and this is true as well of her view of perception, the never-ending commerce between our eyes and the world.

Timothy Findley and Michael Ondaatje occupy the middle section of the study. Here, the postmodernist use of photography is fully articulated, especially in the area of photography's influence on fictional form. Finally, Laurence's more traditional fictional forms and her greater faith in the hegemony of the word bring her into sharp conflict with her postmodernist contemporaries. It is difficult, besides, to resist ending a study of photography and fiction with *The Diviners*, a work which opens with one woman's narrative act: placing photographs in a sequence and translating into words the stories they tell.

Chapter One

✦

"The Delicate Moment of Exposure":
Alice Munro and Photography

The photographer Diane Arbus (1923-71) once cryptically re-marked that "[a] photograph is a secret about a secret. The more it tells you, the less you know" (qtd. in Coleman 77). For Alice Munro, writing, too, involves this delicate balance of conceal-ment and revelation. In "The Ottawa Valley," at the end of her third work, *Something I've Been Meaning to Tell You* (1974), she implicitly comments on these paradoxical ingredients of her fiction, using the analogy of the photograph: "Now I look at what I have done and it is like a series of snapshots, like the brownish snapshots with fancy borders that my parents' old camera used to take" (246). Admitting that her purpose in this collection of stories is to exorcise her mother by forming a clear picture of her – "To mark her off, to describe, to illumine, to celebrate, to *get rid*, of her" – Munro confesses her ultimate failure:

> she looms too close, just as she always did. She is heavy as always, she weighs everything down, and yet she is indistinct, her edges melt and flow. Which means she has stuck to me as close as ever and refused to fall away, and I could go on, and on . . . using what tricks I know, and it would always be the same. (246)

This passage, I would argue, contains within it several elements of Munro's photographic vision: her all-consuming desire for order, her celebration of detail, the conflicts between past and present, fixity and fluidity, and power and helplessness. By studying Munro's evocative and original use of the photograph, we, as readers, may perceive more clearly these elements at work in her fiction; we may learn "a secret about a secret."

Alice Munro has been hailed by various critics as a "realist" (Bowering 4), a "super-realist" (Gervais 9), and a "visionary documentary writer" (Mallinson 70). Each term is related in some way to photography or to twentieth-century photographic realism in the visual arts, and yet each term suggests a widely differing connotation. For George Bowering, Alice Munro belongs to the ranks of "realist" (as opposed to postmodernist) writers who, as Bowering sardonically comments, "tell the normal realist story of sensitive child growing up to be disillusioned but wisely maladjusted adult" (4). Only the postmodernist writer, claims Bowering, shares the photographic vision of a Cartier-Bresson, for whom subject, object, and camera merge in a moment of creation. More recently, in a review of *The Moons of Jupiter* (1982), Alexa DeWiel carries Bowering's denunciation further; Munro is a "superb chronicler of detail," her descriptions are "graphic domestic and geographical," but her characters are "dissected," "analyzed," and finally, "lifeless" (13).

This definition of literary realism – the artist as a mindless cataloguer – proves inadequate when one analyses Munro's treatment of the external world. Indeed, Munro formulates her own defense in a short essay entitled, "What is Real?":

> Yes, I use bits of what is real, in the sense of being really there and really happening, in the world, as most people see it, and I transform it into something that is really there and really happening, in my story. (226)

Thus, there are two levels of reality for Munro; the external reality which serves as a creative stimulus, and the self-contained reality of her fictions. This distinction sheds light on one of Del Jordan's comments in *Lives of Girls and Women* (1971), a comment which has caused some difficulty for critics who see only one level of reality in Munro's creative act. Of her novel-in-progress, Del remarks that "it seemed true to me, not real but true . . . as if that town was lying close behind the one I walked through every day" (248). Or, as Munro comments in "What is Real?": "The fictional room, town, world, needs a bit of starter dough from the real world" (225). Del Jordan receives this "starter dough," this artistic nourishment, from Bobby Sherriff (who appropriately nourishes her in a literal sense as well, by serving her cake and lemonade): "Then he did the only special thing he ever did for me . . . he rose on his toes like a dancer," an act which appears to the apprentice novelist to have "a stylized meaning – to be a letter, or a whole word, in an alphabet I did not know" (253–54). The "real" is, in Del's terms, becoming "true."

Searching for a term which would accord more precisely with Munro's views of realism and reality, critics have turned to the visual arts. "Superrealism," "neorealism," "hyperrealism," "magical realism," and "photographic realism" all refer to a particular school of North American painters – painters of the 1970s and 1980s who have turned from abstraction back to representation (Stevens 64–70). Many of these artists either use or are influenced by photography. American artists Chuck Close and Andy Warhol, for instance, paint supposed "blowups" of photographs, either singly or in series. In Canada, the artists associated with this neo-realist movement include Ken Danby, Christopher Pratt, Jack Chambers, Tom Forrestall, and Alex Colville. When asked by John Metcalf whether she was impressed by Canadian "magic realist" painters such as Forrestall and Colville, Munro replied that she was "very responsive" to their material ("A Conversation" 58). Munro responded in greater detail to Graeme Gibson's question, "Do you see yourself as trying to record things, like a representational painter?", saying that "what I admire is a kind of super realism . . ." When Gibson suggested Andrew Wyeth's name, Munro responded positively, adding the name of Jack Chambers. "[I]t may be," she pondered, "that I'm trying to do this, this same thing" (256).

One senses this shared artistic purpose in a palpable way, when one examines the dust jackets of two of Munro's collections, *Who Do You Think You Are?* (1978) and *The Moons of Jupiter*

(1982). The former features a Ken Danby nude, and the latter a detail from Christopher Pratt's painting, *Young Woman with a Slip*. Apropos of the Pratt painting, Munro told Stephen Scobie in an interview that the Macmillan fiction editor chose the cover painting, but that she personally preferred another Pratt, "a painting I like a lot, with a window and empty shelves" ("A Visit" 12). (Her editor, presumably, feared the addition of visual bleakness to the proverbial "bleakness" of Canadian literature.) Nevertheless, Munro maintained that her favourite Pratt painting forms an analogue to her own style of writing:

> That window picture is more like my stories, because you look out and you see the flat horizon and you see the shades of blue and grey, just flat bars. This one [*Young Woman with a Slip*] is more claustrophobic, and maybe it indicates that most of the stories are about introspective women. (Scobie, "A Visit" 13)

Interestingly, the window-and-shelf motif which Munro prefers is strongly influenced by photography; some of the very earliest daguerrotypes treat a similar subject.

Munro saves her highest praise, however, for the work of an earlier superrealist, Edward Hopper. "I'm crazy about Edward Hopper," she enthusiastically comments to Graeme Gibson (256). Her enthusiasm for Hopper – and for one particular Hopper painting entitled *The Barber Shop* – resurfaces on at least two other occasions. In an interview with John Metcalf, Munro claims that paintings such as this one "do to me exactly the same thing that the writing I respond to does and that I would like to do" ("A Conversation" 58). In "An Open Letter" to *Jubilee*, a Wingham journal named in honour of the fictional town Munro created (a town which is "not 'real,' not on the map, but super-real to me" she said), Munro describes *The Barber Shop* in detail. She claims that the painting describes much better than she ever could the importance which she places on everyday, familiar objects:

> A barber-shop, not yet open; the clock says seven ... fresh morning light of a hot summer day. Beside the barber-shop, a summer-heavy darkness of trees. The plain white slightly shabby barber-shop, so common-

place and familiar; yet everything about in that mild light, is full of a distant, murmuring, almost tender foreboding, full of mystery like the looming trees. (5–7)

The final sentence, with its Conradian rhythms, underlines Munro's purpose: to make us see. Furthermore, this painting, too, is photographic in nature; the surface of the table is cut off by the frame, and the woman does not occupy the central picture space. In terms of composition (though not of execution or of style), it recalls Degas – a painter who actually used photographs as studies for his paintings. It is in this context of photographic superrealism that Munro's work belongs.

Another term which, like "realism," is often misapplied – and has been misapplied to Munro in particular – is "documentary." William H. New refers to the short story "Boys and Girls" from *Dance of the Happy Shades* (1968) as "documenting the family expectations that reinforce traditional roles for boys and girls ..." (*Literary History* 271). The epithet "documentary," however, can be just as derogatory as was the adjective "photographic" for painters in the latter half of the nineteenth century. In a recent article, Catherine Sheldrick Ross places Munro's stories above the level of the documentary, because they are "translations into the next-door language of fiction of all those documentary details" (7). Similarly, John Moss, in *Sex and Violence in the Canadian Novel* (1977), praises Munro's *Lives of Girls and Women* by distinguishing it from the documentary form: "Facts made fiction often more adequately explain reality than document does, coming closer to communicable truth by invention and design than by facsimile reproduction" (61). Ironically, four years later, in *A Reader's Guide to the Canadian Novel* (1981), Moss calls *Lives of Girls and Women* "a document of small-town life during the forties ..." (216).

This confusion stems from the use of one term, "documentary," to refer to two entirely different forms of communication. William Stott, in his detailed and illuminating study, *Documentary Expression and Thirties America* (1973), defines these two species of documentary as, on one hand, the presentation of facts without emotion and, on the other hand, the presentation of the inner life, emotions, or hidden reality. Neither type is fictional; Stott declares that documentary is "fiction's opposite" (xi). Nevertheless, I would argue that the second type of documentary more closely approximates fiction. James Agee and Walker Evans's *Let Us Now Praise Famous Men* (1941), an account in words and photographs of the lives of Alabama tenant farmers in the depression, is much closer to fictional form than other writer-photographer collaborations such as Erskine Caldwell and Margaret Bourke-White's *You Have Seen Their Faces* (1937) – in spite of the fact that Bourke-White was once christened "the poetess of the camera" (216). The reason lies in the relationship between the words and the photographs. Agee claims, in his preface to *Let Us Now Praise Famous Men*, that "[t]he photographs are not illustrative. They, and the text, are coequal, mutually independent, and fully collaborative" (xv). Thus, one *can* read Agee's text without even glancing at Evans's photographs, although the overall impact of the work would, one feels, be greatly diminished.

The impact which this documentary work had on Alice Munro as a young writer was immense. She recently commented to Tim Struthers that she read Agee's other work, *A Death in the Family* (1957), first, and was "*enormously* moved" by Agee's minute descriptions of everyday objects: a pot of water boiling, a curtain moving. Indeed, she praises Agee for his lack of fictionalizing, for his refusal to "manipulate reality instead of letting it dictate by itself what is going to happen in the writing." *Let Us Now Praise Famous Men*, Munro claims, "has things in it which were as important to me as anything I've read" – again, tiny details such as the "texture of the biscuits" Agee eats with one of the sharecropper families. Evans's accompanying photographs she praises for their "artless-seeming" quality (Struthers, "The Real Material" 6–7).

Munro's attraction to Agee and Evans is the attraction of the magical-realist writer to a more magical or imaginative documentary style. Jean Mallinson's description of Munro as a "visionary documentary writer" (70) is not strictly accurate, according to Stott's definition of the document as non-fictional. Rather, one feels that for Munro, the creative process begins on the documentary level – the desire to capture and fix reality – and ends on the imaginative level. For example, Munro claims that her story "Privilege," a largely autobiographical story about Rose's rough-and-tumble school in *Who Do You Think You Are?*, "began ... on a not very deep fictional level, just with the desire, an almost documentary desire .... There's a deeper level that you're not going to when you do that kind of writing, which doesn't mean it isn't valid" (Struthers, "The Real Material" 21). In Munro's world, as I shall discuss, a surface is not merely a surface; it is a reflection of a deeper mystery, either in the perceived world or, more often, within the perceiver. "It was those [ice cream] dishes that told her of her changed stage," we hear of Rose in "Simon's Luck" (170) and "Pots can show malice" towards a younger Rose, receiving a "Royal Beating[s]" from her father, "the patterns of linoleum can leer up at you, treachery is the other side of dailiness" (*Who Do You Think You Are?* 16).

Alice Munro's magical realism, her interest in documentary expression, are parts of a larger whole: her photographic sensibility. Even in the very earliest stages of creation, the story exists for her as a palpable, visual object. "I will be interested [in the story] because of the picture, the image," she told Geoff Hancock, "and then I will just keep finding out more and more about it. But not about the craft, that's the one area where I just never seem to find out anything at all" (85). Like Arbus's photograph, the act of writing proves both revealing and ultimately mysterious to Munro. In "The Colonel's Hash Resettled," a spirited protest against the symbol-hunting tendencies of her critics, Munro traces the growth of her story "Images" from a vision similar to a photographic still-shot:

> It started with the picture in my mind of the man met in the woods [Joe Phippen], coming obliquely down the river-bank, carrying the hatchet, and the child watching him, and the father unaware, bending over his traps . . . .
> From this picture the story moved outward, in a dim uncertain way. ("The Colonel's Hash" 182)

On another occasion, Munro more directly linked her mental vision with photography. When asked how she manages to remember the minute details and textures of the past, Munro replied that "They just come to me when I'm writing. It's a kind of seeing. Last year I saw a black-and-white photo of my high-school class that was taken in Grade Ten, and I *did* remember the color of everyone's clothes" (Murch 70).

In more recent interviews, Munro's comments about photography and its possible relation to her work are more explicit – not necessarily because she has only recently formulated those thoughts, but because the questions of two interviewers in particular, Geoff Hancock and Tim Struthers, are more precise and informed. Indeed, one of Hancock's statements could serve as a prolegomenon to a study such as this one: "I was going to say that controlled mixture of light. The attitude a photographer brings towards the subject. The formal technical process of using a camera are [sic] remarkably similar to the way you use your prose." Munro admitted that photographs are, to her, "very important. I just love looking at them," yet she was less willing to state that her prose can be neatly catalogued: "What I want to get," she claimed, "changes with different stories .... sometimes I want to get something that is very grainy and I don't want any artifice at all," whereas, at other times, she feels that the material demands "a kind of luxuriance" of style (Hancock 107). In fact, this same dichotomy between nature and artifice appears in photography as well. For example, Walker Evans set out to photograph Alabama sharecroppers and their surroundings as simply and as unartificially as he could, as a reaction to Margaret Bourke-White's theatrical snapshots of the South. One account describes Bourke-White photographing a fundamentalist preacher by edging down the central aisle to snap the picture, at a sharp angle, looking upward, and with a blinding flash (Stott 222).

In a revealing conversation with Tim Struthers, Munro claims to be "very interested in photography" and yet is somewhat hesitant about equating writing and photography entirely, for "photographs are too explicit to relate to stories as far as I can see." Nevertheless, when Struthers shifts his line of questioning from questions of strict visual-verbal equations to those of "certain assumptions about life, about the nature of reality" held by photographers such as Evans and Arbus, Munro readily assents to the similarity of their assumptions to her own. Although she denies any intimate knowledge of the assumptions of photographers, saying "I look at the pictures," Munro's claim is certainly a modest one, for she goes on to describe in full detail her "favourite" Diane Arbus photograph, which she admires *"very,* very much." Indeed, her description echoes her evaluation of Edward Hopper's *The Barber Shop,* for here, too, all is literal and mysterious, especially the "very dark border of trees" which surrounds the rather bored-seeming suburban couple (see fig. 1). "It's a very simple photograph," claimed Munro, "with a powerful effect that can't be analyzed, really" (Struthers, "The Real Material" 6). One can hardly imagine a more appropriate description of Munro's own treatment of the "unsatisfactory, apologetic and persistent reality" (Munro, *Dance* 197).

Arbus's photographs, along with those of Walker Evans, have had the greatest impact on Alice Munro. Arbus's work, featuring dwarfs, transvestites, and assorted "freaks," is, to say the least, remote from that of Evans, who photographs poverty-stricken sharecroppers and rickety wooden sheds, yet both photographers have contributed to Munro's vision. It is significant, for instance, that John Reeves chose to photograph Alice Munro sitting in front of a bookshelf upon which stands Arbus's famous photograph of the identical twins. Like Evans's sharecroppers, Arbus's subjects face the camera, dignified in spite of their oddity, just as Evans's subjects retain their dignity in spite of their abject poverty. As Jonathan Lieberson recently wrote of Diane Arbus: "there is no feeling at all that she is setting out to depict freaks. We get instead the impression that she is offering an amused appreciation of people who have chosen to adopt unusual patterns of life" (10). As Munro herself pointed out, Arbus's use of the grotesque is not "fashionable" but "responsible" (Hancock 107). As we shall see, Munro is influenced by both of these opposite poles of photography: Evans's desire to celebrate the familiar, and Arbus's tendency to find the familiar grotesque and the grotesque oddly familiar.

Concurrent with Munro's own elaboration of her ideas about photography is the recent critical attention which has been focused upon this aspect of her writing. Both Joan Coldwell, writing in the *Oxford Companion to Canadian Literature,* and Brandon Conron acknowledge the influence of the photographic realism of James Agee and Eudora Welty upon Munro's style. Tim Struthers, in his article "Alice Munro and the American South," examines closely this influence, claiming that *Lives of Girls and Women* is "a photographer's own documentary." Struthers argues, furthermore, that Munro adopts a "straight, documentary style," revealing "her absolute rejection of the tendency of many photographers to manipulate images" (198).

My reservations about Struthers's argument are two-fold. They concern, first of all, the tendency to describe any fictional work as "documentary," and, second, the assumption that many photographers manipulate reality. In fact, today the work of so-called straight photographers such as Walker Evans and Dorothea Lange (both of whom participated in the Farm Security Administration photography project during the depression) is growing in popularity. These photographers and others such as Ansel Adams and Edward Weston almost unanimously denounced the "literary" or "allegorical" form of photography which became fashionable in the 1860s. Early photographers such as Henry Peach Robinson, in their efforts to make photography respectable and competitive as an art form, attempted to mimic the compositions and subject matters of nineteenth-century painting. A few examples of daguerreotypes from that period are instructive. Swedish photographer Oscar G. Rejlander's *The Two Ways of Life* (1857) shows two young men entering adult life, one inclining towards the allegorical figures of "Religion" and "Charity," the other being led astray by "Gambling," "Wine," and "Licentiousness." (The entire tableau is composed of twenty-five allegorical figures.) Photographers even copied well-known paintings such as Jacques Louis David's *The Oath of the Horatii* (1784); the late nineteenth-century photographic version leaves much to be desired. In this debate, Munro would doubtless side with the "straight" photographers. As we shall see, however, she resolves her distrust of fictionalizing reality by evolving a photographic vision which both mirrors reality and subtly, mysteriously, alters it.

Photographic vision is, by definition, all-inclusive. As Susan Sontag once observed, photography gives us "the sense that we can hold the whole world in our heads – as an anthology of images" (*On Photography* 3). This universal breadth of vision is highly prized by Alice Munro, and so her characters are often shown to be only partially "sighted" beings. For example, in

"The Shining Houses," from *Dance of the Happy Shades*, the selfish younger inhabitants of the new subdivision, who wish to evict Mrs. Fullerton, the owner of an older, ramshackle house, possess a shuttered, partial vision of life. One of these women decides "to draw the drapes" whenever she has visitors, "so they won't see what's across from us" (26). Mary, Mrs. Fullerton's only ally among the suburbanites, strolls down her street and senses the blindness of her neighbours, their "curtains . . . drawn across living-room windows" to "shut off these rooms from the night" (29). The narrator of "The Spanish Lady," from *Something I've Been Meaning to Tell You*, is another character who suffers from partial vision. More pathetic than her failure to perceive the clandestine affair between her husband and her best friend is her failure to recognize a simple act of love performed by her husband many years ago: "That act was like something startling and temporary – a very small bird, say, with rare colours – sitting close by, in a corner of your vision, that you dare not look at openly" (187-88).

In striking contrast to this wilful blindness, Rose, the heroine of *Who Do You Think You Are?*, argues for a vision which is neither shuttered nor peripheral. Remembering the mentally retarded girl who was raped by her brother in the schoolyard, Rose angrily upbraids "[m]en who made books and movies" featuring "the figure of an idiotic, saintly whore," because "[t]hey cheated . . . when they left out the breathing and the spit and the teeth . . ." (26). A vision of life cannot exclude ugliness and pain; as the young girl in "Boys and Girls" comments on the shooting of a farm horse, "It was not something I wanted to see; just the same, if a thing really happened, it was better to see it, and know" (121).

Del Jordan, in *Lives of Girls and Women*, only gradually develops this photographic vision. As a child, Del both desires and fears to witness manifestations of evil or death. The dead cow in the pasture fascinates her, yet on the day of her Uncle Craig's funeral, the dead body is like a "black dot" in a maze which she is desperately trying to avoid (50). Similarly, Del is curiously drawn to the madness and depravity of Uncle Benny's wife, Madeleine, yet when she passes the local bootlegger's house, she is terrified to behold a house which "seemed to embody so much that was evil and mysterious that I would never look at it directly . . ." (7). Later, Del neglects to look directly at her lover Garnet, ignoring the violent streak in him which reasserts itself during the "Baptizing" episode. Even at the end of the epilogue, Del says: "At present I did not look much at this town" (253). Nevertheless, as she listens to Bobby Sherriff, she fixes her gaze on the back wall of a nearby building and notes "certain stains, chipped bricks, a long crack running down diagonally ..." (252). Here is the genesis of the full and honest vision of which Rose speaks. Only from the perspective of the future, however, do we see this mature vision in Del:

> And no list could hold what I wanted, for what I wanted was every last thing, every layer of speech and thought, stroke of light on bark or walls, every smell, pothole, pain, crack, delusion, held still and held together – radiant, everlasting. (253)

One need only compare Del Jordan's artistic manifesto to that of James Agee in *Let Us Now Praise Famous Men* in order to grasp the remarkable similarity of their vision:

> If I could do it, I'd do no writing at all here. It would be photographs; the rest would be fragments of cloth, bits of cotton, lumps of earth, records of speech, pieces of wood and iron, phials of odors, plates of food and of excrement. Booksellers would consider it quite a novelty .... (13)

For Munro, as for Agee, truth must be grounded in physical reality; prosaic, unpleasant, and harsh though it may be.

The inevitable result of this all-inclusive, photographic vision is paradox. The world becomes at once ugly and beautiful, familiar and strange, innocent and threatening. Indeed, Susan Sontag's *On Photography* is couched in terms of paradox: the photograph brings us closer to objective reality and distances us from it; the photograph is both realistic, she argues, and surrealistic (34; 51–52). One often notes the preponderance of paradoxical expressions in criticism and reviews of photography: *Latent Image* (by Beaumont Newhall), "Coolly Obsessed with Humanity" (a review of Cartier-Bresson's photographs), "dispassionately passionate" (a comment on Richard Kirstel's photographs by photography critic A.D. Coleman). This fascination with paradox – in fact with the very same paradoxes which surround photography – is a central characteristic of Alice Munro's fiction.

One of the most consistent and glaring paradoxes in Munro's work is the fact that ordinary objects may inspire both reverence and suspicion. In "Images," Del's description of her father's work boots is both a celebration and a revelation:

> His boots were to me as unique and familiar, as much an index to himself as his face was. When he had taken them off they stood in a corner of the kitchen, giving off a complicated smell of manure, machine oil, caked black mud, and the ripe and disintegrating material that lined their soles. They were a part of himself, temporarily discarded, waiting. (*Dance* 36)

One wonders whether Munro was influenced by a similar photographic celebration: Walker Evans's photograph of a pair of worn, mud-caked work boots in *Let Us Now Praise Famous Men* (see fig. 2) – itself a visual quotation of Vincent van Gogh's *Boots*, 1887. Certainly, this celebration of prosaic articles is a feature of the documentary photographs of Evans and of Lewis Hine. Hine, well known for his photographs of working men and women, is also known for quoting George Eliot's discussion of "the faithful representation of everyday things" at a conference of "Charities and Corrections" in Buffalo in 1909:

> Do not impose on us any aesthetic rules which shall banish from the reign of art those old women with work-worn hands scraping carrots ... those rounded backs and weather-beaten faces that have bent over the spade and done the rough work of the world, those homes with their tin pans, their brown pitchers, their rough curs and their clusters of onions. (Gutman 29)

This reverence toward everyday objects frequently appears in Munro's characters, in their belief that external objects can somehow "save" them. The narrator of "An Ounce of Cure," after her first bout with the adult compound, whisky, stares gratefully at "the little six-sided white tiles, which lay together in such an admirable and logical pattern" on the bathroom floor

(*Dance* 81). Del Jordan, after a similar overindulgence at the notorious Gay-la Dance Hall, feels "redeemed by childish things – my old Scarlett O'Hara lamp, the blue and white metal flowers that held back my limp dotted curtains" (*Lives* 193–94). Again, note the religious term "redeemed." Later, as a student, Del worships the objects which she fixes in her mind: "verbs, dates, wars, phyla" which "took on a significance, an admonitory power, as if all these ordinary shapes and patterns of things were in fact the outward form of the facts and relationships which I had mastered, and which, once I had mastered them, came to seem lovely, chaste, and obedient" (208).

For Munro's characters, however, objects simply refuse to remain "lovely, chaste, and obedient"; more often, they reveal unsuspected levels of treachery. Rose, like the narrator of "An Ounce of Cure," fixes her eyes upon the "comforting geometrical arrangement" of the floor tiles in "Royal Beatings," only to discover, to her profound shock, that "[t]hose things aren't going to help her, none of them can rescue her. They turn bland and useless, even unfriendly" (*Who* 16). An older Rose senses this same latent treachery in objects; after her night-long vigil, waiting for her lover's return in "Simon's Luck," she peevishly blames the wine, sheets, cheese, and cherries which she has bought for the occasion: "Preparations court disaster" she wryly reflects (166). Only later, while staring at the ice-cream dishes "that told her of her changed state" (that is, no longer in love), does Rose shift the blame from external objects to her internal weakness, her inflexibility: "the surprise was that she so much wanted, required, everything to be there for her, thick and plain as ice-cream dishes . . . " (170). Rose must, in short, learn to trust the internal and complex as well as the external and simple. As Rose reflects of her acting career, "she might have been paying attention to the wrong things, reporting antics, when there was always something further, a tone, a depth, a light that she couldn't get and wouldn't get" (205).

The prosaic object is often dangerous for Munro's characters because it demands or inevitably entails an emotional response. When Mr. Malley in "The Office" offers the young writer various objects to put in her new office – a teapot, wastebasket, plant – the writer perceives these gifts as a form of emotional blackmail. "I had not planned," she emphatically states, "in taking an office, to take on the responsibility of knowing any more human beings" (*Dance* 64). Such an admission, issuing from the mouth of a writer, is clearly ironic. Similarly, in "Day of the Butterfly," the young narrator sees the gifts which her classmates have hypocritically bestowed upon Myra Sayla, their unpopular, mistreated classmate, as "guilt-tinged offerings": "They were no longer innocent objects to be touched, exchanged, accepted without danger" (*Dance* 110). When Myra attempts one such emotional exchange, by giving the narrator one of these gifts, the narrator avoids the dangers of human sympathy; she indifferently shrugs off the gift as "the thing." The older, maturer voice of the narrator, however, assures us that, for her, as for Rose, the danger lies not in the physical object, but in "the treachery of my own heart" (110).

This association between objects and guilt or danger lies deep in Munro's own mind, and has, for her, a direct relation to photography. In the autobiographical "Boys and Girls," Munro's young protagonist associates her disobedience in letting the horse run free, with the sight of the coat which her brother wore on that fateful day:

> But whenever I saw the brown and white checked coat hanging in the closet, or at the bottom of the rag bag, which was where it ended up, I felt a weight in my stomach, the sadness of un-exorcized guilt. (*Dance* 123)

In her personal memoir of her father, "Working for a Living," Munro reveals this same association between visualized object and powerful past emotion. While driving on the rural roads of Bruce County with her husband, Munro recalls seeing "a country store with long, old-fashioned window-panes . . . I felt that I had seen the store before and I connected it with a disappointment" (18). Little by little, Munro recalls the disappointing ice-cream cone her father bought for her at that very store when she was a child (disappointing because it contained splinters of ice), until she uncovers the true source of her sadness; that her father had taken this unfrequented route because he had no money to repair his car and it could therefore have broken down at any moment. It is no wonder, then, that Munro speaks with such conviction of "a sort of treachery to innocent objects – to houses, chairs, dresses, dishes, and to roads, fields, landscapes – which a writer removes from their natural, dignified obscurity and sets down in print" (181–82). Munro then relates this treachery of the artistically rendered object to the power of photography to reveal hidden depths: "[t]here are primitive people who will not allow themselves to be photographed for fear the camera will steal their souls. That has always seemed to me a not unreasonable belief" ("The Colonel's Hash" 182).

Closely related to this photographic paradox of reverence and fear of the object is the paradox of surfaces and depths which also runs through Munro's fiction. Like Margaret Atwood in "This Is a Photograph of Me," Munro is constantly challenging her reader to look beyond the surface, to discover the mystery inherent in the prosaic. Although Munro has commented to Graeme Gibson that she is "very, very excited by what you might call the surface of life" (Gibson 241), she agreed readily when John Metcalf asked her, "do you feel 'surfaces' not to *be* surfaces?" ("A Conversation" 56). Munro's work both bears out this paradoxical attitude and relates it explicitly to photography. In *Lives of Girls and Women*, the photograph of Marion Sherriff which hangs in the main hall of the school reveals a "stocky and unsmiling" girl holding a tennis racket, but conceals the mystery of her subsequent suicide (244). One is reminded of the concern with surfaces and depths shown in the earliest North American novel to deal with photography as a metaphor, Nathaniel Hawthorne's *The House of the Seven Gables* (1851), in which Holgrave, the photographer, comments on his daguerreotypes: "There is a wonderful insight in heaven's broad and simple sunshine. While we give it credit only for depicting the merest surface, it actually brings out the secret character with a truth that no painter would ever venture upon, even if he could detect it" (68).

For Munro, the depths which are hidden by the small-town "surfaces" are frequently grotesque: witness the drowning of Miss Farris in *Lives of Girls and Women*, or the hideous illness of the narrator's mother in "The Peace of Utrecht" – a hideousness which both the narrator and her sister Maddy attempt to conceal beneath the orderly, brisk surface of their daily lives. Nevertheless, this view represents only one side of the paradoxical vision which Munro – like photographers such as Arbus – possesses: that the familiar is grotesque and the grotesque is familiar. In "The Peace of Utrecht," for example, Maddy and Helen's attempt to hide their mother from the town is more grotesque, at heart, than their mother's illness. "We should have let the town have her," the narrator bitterly reflects, "it would have treated her better" (*Dance* 195). Indeed, the dim-witted Milton Homer in *Who Do You Think You Are?* finds ready acceptance in the town of Hanratty: "Nobody looked askance at Milton in a parade; everybody was used to him" (193). Years later, when an outsider, Rose's sister-in-law Phoebe, tries to understand what sort of character Milton Homer was, she resorts to sophisticated cliché, "[t]he village idiot," and Rose and her brother claim that "they had never heard him described that way" (193). Munro has often defended her characters against reviewers who, like Phoebe, exclaim at the grotesque or arid quality of the small town in her works. In *Jubilee*, for instance, she maintains that "It is not true that such a place will not allow eccentricity. Oddity is necessary, just as much as sin is; it is just that both things must be classified, and declared and appreciated." Indeed, Munro affectionately speaks of the lives of her characters in paradoxical terms; they are both "buried and celebrated" ("An Open Letter" 5–6).

This paradoxical vision, whereby the buried may be celebrated and the grotesque may be beautiful, is essentially a photographic vision. Indeed, the photograph's tendency to bestow formal beauty on the most horrifying of subject matter has troubled photographers and critics alike. Of a 1969 exhibition of photographs from Harlem, A.D. Coleman maintained that the photographer had:

> transmuted a truth which is not beautiful into an art which is. If the reality on which that beauty is based were transmuted at the same time, I would have no objections, but it is not . . . This is one of the paradoxes of contemporary documentary photography. (47)

Marxist critics of photography such as Walter Benjamin see this beautification of the ugly as a means of pacifying antiestablishment criticism. Thus, photographer Franz-Roh's response to the Bauhaus photographers' anthology, *The World is Beautiful* (1928), resembles in intent Munro's fiction: "our book does not only mean to say 'the world is beautiful,' but also: the world is

exciting, cruel and weird" (qtd. in Watney 167). For Alice
Munro, as for many photographers, both propositions are true.

"Epilogue: The Photographer" in *Lives of Girls and Women* is
Munro's most systematic and sustained attempt to describe the
paradoxes of surfaces and depths, and of the familiar and the
grotesque, using the metaphor of photography. Many critics
seem puzzled, however, as to the nature of the mysterious
photographer figure who haunts the melodramatic fragments of
Del's imagined novel. Antony B. Dawson calls the photographer "a kind of sinister image of the sort of artist that Del wants
to be" (58), and Tim Struthers describes his photographs as
"false notions of reality" which Del eventually repudiates
("Reality and Ordering" 46). John Moss in *Sex and Violence in the
Canadian Novel* is virtually alone in perceiving a positive link
between Del and the photographer. His photographs, says
Moss, are "darkly prophetic and photographically vivid. Del
will be an artist in the same mold." He qualifies this last
statement, however, by commenting that Del's "visions will be
prophetic in a different way, though, due to the point of view
from which they are seen" (60). Moss, I feel, is right in his
opinion of the photographer, yet his qualifications are vague
and unsatisfactory. In what sense will Del's visions be different?
How will the creator's or the observer's point of view change?

First of all, the photographer's pictures are not "fictive," as
Struthers argues; they have not "distorted life, instead of
revealing it" ("Alice Munro" 202). Indeed, the opposite is true;
the photographs reveal what is present – whether in the past or
in the future – or what is potentially true:

> The pictures he took turned out to be unusual, even
> frightening. People saw that in his pictures they had
> aged twenty or thirty years. Middle-aged people saw in
> their own features the terrible, growing, inescapable
> likeness of their dead parents; young fresh girls and
> men showed what gaunt or dulled or stupid faces they
> would have when they were fifty. Brides looked preg-
> nant, children adenoidal. (*Lives* 246–47)

The truth which the photographer reveals, Munro emphasizes,
is an unpleasant but "inescapable" one. In fact, her further
comment, "[s]o he was not a popular photographer ..." (247),

could be applied to Munro's own unsteady relations with the inhabitants of her transformed town, Wingham, Ontario.

The perspective which Del's photographer lacks – the "point of view" to which Moss perhaps refers – is the ability to see the other half of the paradox of the grotesque and the beautiful. Caroline, Del's lovely heroine, pursues the photographer and offers herself to him, just as objective reality offers itself to the photographer or to the writer. The relationship bears fruit; Caroline's womb is, in Del's melodramatic and mawkish prose, "swollen *like a hard yellow gourd in her belly* . . . " (247). Even this promise of fruitfulness, however, turns sour; the photographer's car overturns (significantly, beside a "dry creek" [247]), and Caroline commits suicide. The photographer, then, although he is adept at uncovering the grotesque secrets of the town, cannot conceive of any sort of positive creation. Munro, it would seem, is issuing an artistic manifesto, differentiating herself from the fictional "photographers" of small towns such as Sherwood Anderson, writers who can only perceive one side of the paradox of ugliness and beauty. "All the men and women the writer had ever known had become grotesques," writes Anderson in *Winesburg, Ohio* (1919 [3]). For Alice Munro, as for Diane Arbus, all the grotesques she has ever known become men and women.

Del's view, then, encompasses that of her photographer, just as her new novel will be not as much a repudiation of the vision in her gothic novel, as an inclusion of the beauties as well as the grotesqueries of reality. Instead of the "darker, more decaying town" (247) of her first novel, she will create a Jubilee which is at once "dull, simple, amazing and unfathomable," where every homely detail, "every smell, pothole, pain, crack, delusion" will become "radiant, everlasting" (253). The symbol of Del's maturer vision is the photograph of Marion Sherriff (the model for Del's fictional Caroline) which undergoes a transformation in Del's mind, as she listens to Bobby Sherriff: "Her face was stubborn, unrevealing, lowered so that shadows had settled in her eyes" (253). This progressive darkening of Marion's eyes contrasts sharply with the condition of Caroline's eyes, as revealed by Del's photographer: *"Caroline's eyes were white"* (247). This image of white becoming dark – the photographic transformation from a negative to a positive image – suggests the completeness of Del's vision. She will reveal and

unmask reality, like her photographer, but she will also celebrate it, create it, and render it more complex, adding delicate
shadows to stark reality.

✤ ✤ ✤

Susan Sontag once wrote: "All photographs are *memento mori*.
To take a photograph is to participate in another person's (or
thing's) mortality, vulnerability, mutability." Paradoxically, she
continues, by capturing a moment of life, one emphasizes that
that particular moment has vanished forever (*On Photography*
15). This double consciousness pervades most of the literature
which deals with photography; witness Philip Larkin's "Lines
on a Young Lady's Photograph Album":

> How overwhelmingly persuades
> That this is a real girl in a real place
> In every sense empirically true!
> Or is it just *the past*?

(Larkin 232–33)

Alice Munro – a writer who constantly attempts to recreate the
atmosphere and texture of the past – uses photography as an
analogous means of bringing together the past and the present.
In "Something I've Been Meaning to Tell You," Et is astonished,
looking at a photograph of her sister Char, to discover that
"Char was beautiful" (*Something* 5). Moving from the past
image to the present – Char scrubbing in the kitchen – Et
recognizes both the superficial change in her sister and "the
same almost disdainful harmony" in Char's face "as in the
photograph." Past and present, then, are not to be easily
categorized, set apart from each other; like Del's photographer,
Et realizes that "the qualities of legend were real, that they
surfaced where and when you least expected" (6).

Munro has commented that she likes "looking at people's
lives over a number of years, without continuity. Like catching
them in snapshots. And I like the way people relate, or don't
relate, to the people they were earlier" (Hancock 89). The
narrator of "The Turkey Season" from *The Moons of Jupiter* finds
herself in the latter predicament when she looks at a photograph of herself as part of a turkey-barn crew. Munro actually

40

owns such a photograph of the workers at the turkey barn which her father owned. She found the photograph, she told Stephen Scobie, while going through her father's effects. That detail, as well as the fact that she mentions "Working for a Living," her memoir of her father, immediately after this comment, suggests that creating a story from this visual artifact involves the recreation of a deeply personal past, and an attempt to immortalize the mortal and the transitory (Scobie, "A Visit" 13). Of the fictional photograph, the narrator of her story reflects: "I am stout and cheerful and comradely in the picture, transformed into someone I don't ever remember being or pretending to be" (72). Not only is the narrator distanced from her past visually but emotionally and intellectually as well. Now, she assumes that the turbulence in the group of workers was probably caused by sexual jealousy (a woman and a man competing for the favours of the male boss). Even so, her knowledge can never be entirely satisfying. "I would still like to know things," she claims, "[n]ever mind facts. Never mind theories either" (74). Knowledge of the past, Munro implies, is not a matter of verification or theorizing; like the iconic photograph, the past – and all its levels of meaning – defeats us.

Sometimes, Munro uses the photograph to emphasize the bizarre dislocation between the past and the present. This association is by no means unusual. Photographer Jean Mohr has written:

A photograph arrests the flow of time in which the event photographed once existed. All photographs are of the past, yet in them an instant of the past is arrested so that, unlike a lived past, it can never lead to the present. Every photograph presents us with two messages: a message concerning the event photographed and another concerning a shock of discontinuity. (Berger and Mohr 86)

In "Privilege," from *Who Do You Think You Are?*, Rose sees West Hanratty as two photographs, one taken before the war and the other after: "it was as if an entirely different lighting had been used, or as if it was all on film and the film had been printed in a different way, so that on the one hand things looked clean-edged and decent and limited and ordinary, and on the

41

other, dark, grainy, jumbled, and disturbing" (37). The different materials which produce such varied effects represent, of course, the changing consciousness of the child who begins to perceive the undercurrents of violence and hostility in the town (and, more particularly in "Privilege," in the school).

A similar dislocation between past and present is perceived by the narrator of "Material" from *Something I've Been Meaning to Tell You*, when she gazes at the photograph of her ex-husband Hugo in a collection of short stories:

> He looked, however, very much as I would have thought he would look by now .... I had foreseen the ways in which time and his life would have changed him .... Pouches under his eyes, a dragged-down look to the cheeks even when he is laughing. He is laughing, into the camera. His teeth have gone from bad to worse. He hated dentists, said his father died of a heart attack in the dentist's chair. A lie, like so much else, or at least an exaggeration. He used to smile crookedly for photographs to hide the right top incisor .... (28)

The photograph of Hugo, like Diane Arbus's photographs, both reveals and conceals. Although he is facing the camera – a pose which in Arbus's photographs, for instance, suggests unashamed self-revelation – he is implicitly concealing or falsifying the past. The narrator knows the truth about his insecurities, such as his hatred of dentists; she knows all of the "lies, the half-lies, the absurdities" which make up Hugo's personality. Noting the checked wool shirt and the undershirt which Hugo sports in this photograph, the narrator senses that Hugo is attempting to create a false image of the writer as a carefree lumberjack. Indignantly, she orders us to "[l]ook at Hugo's picture, look at the undershirt," and to compare the façade which we see there and in Hugo's pretentious author's "blurb" with the insecure and domineering man she knew in the past. This disjunction between past and present is further intensified when the narrator admits that her knowledge of Hugo's present life, pieced together from the scanty evidence offered by the photograph, is woefully inadequate: "I have no proof. I construct somebody from this one smudgy picture, I am content with such clichés" (29). The photograph, then, points to a truth about human nature which Hugo misses entirely in his story about Dotty, the "harlot-in-residence" in their old apartment building: that knowledge of external appearances is a flimsy excuse for knowledge of the internal, mysterious workings of the mind and of the past (31). The narrator thus rejects Hugo's flimsy excuse for fiction – his use of Dotty as "material": *"This is not enough, Hugo. You think it is, but it isn't. You are mistaken, Hugo"* (44). The photograph, as an analogue to Hugo's fictional distortion of the past, assists both the narrator and the reader to this final decision.

Munro often uses a particular type of photograph – the family photograph – to study the paradoxical disjunction *and* continuity between the past and the present. Nora, Ben Jordan's former girlfriend in "Walker Brothers Cowboy" from *Dance of the Happy Shades*, weakly tries to bridge the gulf between the past she shared with Ben and her lonely present, by showing him family photographs. When he sees a photograph of Nora's sister, Ben protests that he "can't think of her any way but when she was going to school" (14), a prophetic sign of his unwillingness to bring Nora herself into his present life. In *Lives of Girls and Women*, another character who belongs entirely to the past, Uncle Craig, is associated with photographs – one of a pioneering log cabin, and another, a family portrait in which his sisters, Aunt Elspeth and Aunt Grace, "sat on hassocks at his head and feet," as though he were an idol. The young Craig appears "self-satisfied" and pampered and Del marvels that the aunts spoke of him "as if he were still that boy, stretched out there in beguiling insolence, for them to pamper and laugh at" (29). Thus the aunts, like Craig, with his devotion to his history of Wawanash County, are entirely caught up in the past. They appropriately act as messengers from the past, handing down to Del the incomplete manuscript of Craig's history, which Del does not yet appreciate – the record of "the whole solid, intricate structure of lives supporting us from the past" (31).

Often photographs themselves are associated with such a reevaluation of the past. The narrator of "Winter Wind" from *Something I've Been Meaning to Tell You* pays no attention to a photograph of her grandmother, Aunt Madge, great aunts, and great-grandparents, until her grandmother dies and Aunt Madge is taken to a nursing home. Then, she tells us: "I salvaged it, and have taken it with me wherever I go." The photograph becomes a talisman, a protection against mortality. Furthermore, the narrator's detailed description of the portrait-sitters reveals the value of the link with the past which she has just discovered. Of her great-grandfather the narrator claims: "This photograph was the sign and record of his achievement: respectability, moderate prosperity, mollified wife in a black silk dress, the well-turned-out tall daughters." This statement presents the family as it would wish to appear. Nevertheless, the narrator then examines more imaginatively, more probingly, the truth beneath this ordered surface: the dresses actually look "frightful"; Aunt Madge has probably had to make her sisters' dresses; there is something "askew" at the waist of the grandmother's dress (194); the grandmother herself seems "askew," for she appears upon closer scrutiny to have "no authority," to be "shamefaced," and a "great tomboy" (195). In short, the narrator perceives the truth of the past, imperfect as it is, and this imperfection renders it all the more personal and intimate to her. Thus, Brandon Conron's belief that this photograph "symbolizes the personal sacrifices made by her ancestors to carve out an ordered way of life" is only partially true (121). The narrator, by perceiving the truth beyond the surface of the photograph, realizes the sacrifices which these people have made, but realizes as well that their "way of life" was not as "ordered" as she initially believed.

Munro's acute consciousness of human transience is closely connected with yet another paradox in her art – the paradox of control and helplessness, fixity and flux. As she commented to Graeme Gibson about her writing: "With me it has something to do with the fight against death, the feeling that we lose everything every day, and writing is a way of convincing yourself perhaps that you're doing something about this. You're not really, because the writing itself does not last much longer than you do ... " (243). For many photographers, too, this attempt to fix external reality is the *raison d'être* of their art; as French photographer Cartier-Bresson says, he wants "to find the structure of the world – to revel in the pure pleasure of form," to show that "in all this chaos, there is order" (qtd. in Sontag, *On Photography* 100). Nevertheless, if the photographer holds the power to render immortal what is momentary, he or she is still dependent on what is *there* to be photographed, external reality. Thus, the ultimate impossibility of the camera ever achieving this supreme control over the minutiae of experience is contained in Susan Sontag's paradoxical christening of photography as the "assault on reality and submission to reality" (*On Photography* 123).

Frequently, Munro's characters reach this same insight into the helplessness which underlies all of their attempts to order and control the external world. Del, in *Lives of Girls and Women*, for instance, follows up her catalogue of details which she hopes to enshrine forever in her fiction, with the rueful admission: "The hope of accuracy we bring to such tasks is crazy, heartbreaking" (253). Similarly, the photograph of Et which Arthur keeps on his bureau, from "Something I've Been Meaning to Tell You," represents an attempt to order his memory of his late wife. Instead of recognizing the chaos which existed within Et and which finally culminated in her suicide, Arthur prefers to see her as she appears in the photograph: "in her costume for that play, where she played the statue-girl" – an example of fixity, indeed (23). In *Who Do You Think You Are?*, Rose's husband, Patrick, betrays this same pathetic desire to "fix" his wife; when it becomes apparent that Rose wants a divorce, she discovers Patrick one day "putting fresh Scotch tape on the snapshots in the album." This attempt to control what is no longer controllable can only fail; Rose, whose perception of Patrick and of the marriage is finally clear, sees these photographs of happier domestic times for what they are, "true lies" (133). Munro's attitude towards the photograph's – and man's – vain attempt to control recalcitrant reality thus echoes that of Benedetto Croce: "And if photography be not quite an art, that is precisely because the element of nature in it remains more or less unconquered and ineradicable" (qtd. in Sekula 102).

The photograph is the meeting place not only of power and helplessness, the familiar and the grotesque, but of motion and stillness as well. It is the static moment snatched out of the *perpetuum mobile* of time – what Cartier-Bresson termed "the decisive moment." In Alice Munro's fiction, too, the "moment" is often "decisive," often given the importance of a still-shot in film. For example, Del in "Images" attests to the crucial importance of her meeting with Old Joe Phippen; she becomes "like a child in an old negative, electrified against the dark noon sky, with blazing hair and burned-out Orphan Annie eyes" (*Dance* 38). She is "transfixed" – a word which suggests, as does the image of the photographic negative, a ceasing of the normal time sequence. Since Joe himself represents all that is weird and terrifying, hidden under the surface, this interruption of the time sequence of ordinary life is certainly appropriate.

Munro frequently emphasizes this sense of the momentary by using the word "exposure" – a term suggesting both revelation and the photographic moment. The young girl in "An Ounce of Cure" fears the personal "exposure" which has been the result of her debauch – the momentary relaxing of her emotional guard. On a higher level, the narrator of "The Office" associates exposure with the ultimate act of revelation, writing: "However I put it, the words create their space of silence, the delicate moment of exposure" (*Dance* 59). Munro herself uses the term a great deal in reference to her writing. The inhabitants of Wingham, she claims in "What Is Real?", fear what they see as Munro's "deliberate exposure" of the town (225). Moreover, she confessed to Graeme Gibson that she must not think of writing for a particular audience, because if she did "the sense of self-exposure" would be overwhelming (253). Thus, in theory and practice, Munro is fascinated by a type of momentary self-revelation, similar to the instantaneous "exposure" of the camera.

In her fiction, however, she often juxtaposes the "decisive moment" with the motion and continuum of life – yet another paradox. In *Who Do You Think You Are?*, this pattern is often repeated; Rose, watching Patrick in his library carrel, adopts the stance of the detached observer: "she was free. She could look at him as she would look at anybody" (93). She does not, however, remain an observer for long. She has "a compelling picture of herself" running into Patrick's carrel and embracing him, almost in the manner of a film sequence. The picture swiftly becomes reality, however, when we are suddenly told: "She did it" (94). This interplay between stasis and continuum reinforces the fact that Rose often finds herself dragged along

46

by the force of events in her life. Another example is her aimless and obsessive drive through Ontario and Manitoba after she is deserted by her lover, Simon. When Rose discovers, years later, that Simon deserted her because he found out that he had cancer, she explicitly ponders the relationship between momentary events and the film-like continuum of our lives: "People watching [film] trusted that they would be protected from predictable disasters, also from those shifts of emphasis that throw the story line open to question, the disarrangements which demand new judgments and solutions ..." (172-73). Rose is beginning at last to understand the paradox of life which T.S. Eliot called "[t]he point of intersection of the timeless / With time ..." ("The Dry Salvages" 198).

This passage from *Who Do You Think You Are?* with its Eliot-like message throws light on another scene where Munro juxtaposes motion and stasis. At the end of "The Time of Death," from *Dance of the Happy Shades*, the photographic image of the dilapidated wooden buildings is suddenly animated: "The snow came, falling slowly, evenly ..." (99). As Tim Struthers comments, "she presents a still photograph which, with the final detail of the snowfall, evolves into a film" ("Alice Munro" 198). Struthers does not mention the function of this transformation, but certainly the death of the child Benny could be one of the "predictable disasters" or "disarrangements" of which Rose speaks. In this instance, too, as in Rose's life, the "film" of life must continue, absorbing as well as it can these dislocations of the story-line. "What's life?" asks Leona Parry in the same story. "You gotta go on" (98). Nevertheless, the momentary event affects deeply the continuum of one's life; Patricia Parry goes on, but continues to carry inside her the burden of guilt for her brother's death. As Eliot remarks in "The Dry Salvages" – in lines which echo Munro's concerns and which probably provided her with the title of her story:

At the moment which is not of action or inaction
You can receive this: "on whatever sphere of being
The mind of a man may be intent
At the time of death" – that is the one action
(And the time of death is every moment)
Which shall fructify in the lives of others. (197)

✦ ✦ ✦

A final consideration in studying Alice Munro's use of photography is the extent to which the photograph has influenced the form of her fiction. Titles such as "Images" and "Red Dress: 1946" certainly recall photographs. Beyond this similarity, the very concept of a series of short stories is associated in Munro's mind with a type of photographic vision of life. She once commented about *Who Do You Think You Are?*:

> I think there are flickerings of self-knowledge or maturity in and out throughout your life, there isn't a plateau which people reach and then remain [sic]. Those clichés that as you get older, you get wiser aren't necessarily true, there are peaks and hollows all along the way. (McNeilly 74)

More recently, Munro has reiterated this idea, saying: "There are just flashes of things we know and find out. I don't see life very much in terms of progress" (Hancock 102). Critics, too, have used language remarkably similar to Munro's in defining the form of her stories. John Moss, for instance, describes Munro transcending time by recording the "brilliant flashes" of experience (*Sex and Violence* 56).

The interconnected short story form, such as one finds in *Who Do You Think You Are?* and to a lesser extent in *Lives of Girls and Women*, is perfectly suited to Munro's conception of human maturity. As Tim Struthers commented in a review of *Who Do You Think You Are?*, its storyline is "a moving picture presented by means of multiple exposures" (5). In fact, Susan Sontag has described the photographic conception of the world as "a series of unrelated, freestanding particles" (*On Photography* 23). Critics of Munro, however, continue to expect her "freestanding particles" of fiction to function as a novel. For example, Carole Gerson referred, in an interview with Munro, to the "gaps" in *Who Do You Think You Are?*, to which Munro responded, "I think you're looking at it as a failed novel ... " (4). Several stories in the collection present characters who do not resurface in a major way in the other stories; for instance, Rose's daughter Anna in "Providence," Simon in "Simon's Luck," and Clifford and Jocelyn in "Mischief." The self-sufficiency of these stories supports the idea that the collection is a group of selected moments from Rose's life – a sort of emotional photograph album.

One finds explicit support for this conception of Munro's collections in two passages from her work. In *Lives of Girls and Women*, Del attempts to construct a mental photograph album in which she might collect and reconcile her conflicting perceptions of Miss Farris, the teacher who commits suicide:

> Miss Farris in her velvet skating costume . . . Miss Farris *con brio*, Miss Farris painting faces in the Council Chambers, Miss Farris floating face down, unprotesting, in the Wawanash River, six days before she was found. Though there is no plausible way of hanging those pictures together – if the last one is true then must it not alter the others? – they are going to have to stay together now. (141)

This passage reproduces the form of *Lives of Girls and Women* in miniature. Each phase of Del's life – her religious experimentation, her sexual curiosity, her fear of death – is one picture which must be "hung" along with the others if we are to gain an honest insight into the maturing mind of a young artist. Moreover, Del's comment about the last picture of Miss Farris inevitably influencing the others reveals a curious truth about Del's own story. The epilogue, which directly treats Del's ambition to be a writer, causes the reader to return to the earlier stories in *Lives of Girls and Women* (even if only mentally) to reconsider the earlier evidence of Del's sensitivity to language and experience. *Lives of Girls and Women* is thus the fictional photograph album of a young artist.

A similar passage, in which Munro explicitly refers to a collection of stories as a series of photographs, is the ending of "The Ottawa Valley" from *Something I've Been Meaning to Tell You*. The narrator surveys the "series of snapshots" – her story – in which almost all the subjects, her Aunt Dodie, Uncle James, Aunt Lena, "come out clear enough," except for her mother, whose "edges melt and flow" (246). The placing of this story at the very end of the collection suggests that the metaphor of the series of snapshots applies to the entire collection. Lorna Irvine, although she accepts this idea, claims that the content of

49

Something I've Been Meaning to Tell You cannot very successfully be compared to snapshots, because "[t]he boundaries of these women [the narrators and characters of the other stories] are not clear" (102). Nevertheless, one might argue that no central female character in Munro's stories is simple (not even the young girls in "How I Met My Husband" and "An Ounce of Cure"). In addition, the image of the photograph, as we have seen, does not necessarily imply a fully successful ordering or capturing of reality, but a dialectic of power and helplessness. Munro's narrator fittingly concludes her artistic manifesto by declaring: "I could go on, and on, applying what skills I have, using what tricks I know, and it would always be the same" (246). In the context of Munro's fiction, "tricks" often refers to fictional technique; the narrator of "Material," for example, praises Hugo's story for its "Lovely tricks, honest tricks" (*Something* 43). Thus, the links between the series of "brownish snapshots" and Munro's short story collection are extremely strong. In fact, the passage from "The Ottawa Valley" virtually echoes American photographer W. Eugene Smith's definition of a photo-essay: "You keep working out the relationships between the people, and you look back at the relationships you have established . . . . There should be a coherence between the pictures" (Hill and Cooper 266).

Alice Munro's paradoxical vision of human experience is the basis for her fascination with the photographic image. The photograph miraculously contains within it beauty, ugliness, the familiar, the grotesque, the past, the present, motion, stasis, comfort, and treachery. It thus becomes the perfect vehicle for probing lives which are, in Munro's own words, "Solitary and meshed . . . buried and celebrated." In fact, the closing sentences of William Stott's book on the documentary form unwittingly sum up Munro's attitude towards the burials and celebrations of human life: "That the world can be improved and yet must be celebrated as it is are contradictions. The beginning of maturity may be the recognition that both are true" (314). By carefully framing and ordering her perceptions upon the delicate lens of her prose, Alice Munro brings us one step closer to that maturity.

Chapter Two

✚

" Violent Stillness ":
Timothy Findley's
Use of Photography

Cassandra Wakelin, the heroine of Timothy Findley's play, *Can You See Me Yet?* (1977), finds herself in the "Ontario Asylum for the Insane" with only one symbol of order, identity, and the past to cling to: a photograph album. By imagining her fellow inmates to be members of her family, acting out traumatic moments from the past, Cassandra painfully assembles her own mental photograph album. Her gradual reacquaintance with her past is crushed, however, when an inmate reveals the truth about her album: "It isn't yours! It's all a lie!" (146). Another inmate defends Cassandra's adoption of the photographs, and in so doing champions the triumph of fiction over mere fact:

> If she says the book's the story of her life, then it's the story of her life. And if it is, she's lucky, even if she stole it. I wish someone would go back out and steal a story of my life. My life doesn't have a story. Otherwise, I wouldn't be here. (148)

This scene reproduces in miniature the two conflicting attitudes toward the photograph which one finds at various stages in Timothy Findley's writing career. Unlike Alice Munro, who sees photography as a symbol of the celebration of prosaic reality, Findley emphasizes, especially in earlier works, the darker elements associated with the camera image: artificiality, lies, stifling fixity, and even fascism. Only in more recent works, beginning with *Can You See Me Yet?* and *The Wars* (1977), has Findley come to appreciate the photograph as an invaluable preserver of the past as well as an image of what he called "violent stillness"(*The Last of the Crazy People* 279).

Findley's responses to the photograph differ from Munro's largely because of his very different experiences with visual images. He has been in various periods of his life a painter, a dancer, an actor, a playwright, and a screenwriter as well as a novelist, and in each of those endeavours he has shown a marked preference for expressing motion rather than fixity. As a painter, for instance, Findley favours human subjects over still life or landscape – human subjects caught up in the process of living, "occupied with something private" while they are in physical "repose," caught "in a particular moment of their life – or their day . . . ." He emphasizes that he does not approach a portrait as a static study of "the person's face," but as a glimpse of "the attitude of the person who was sitting there." Even the canvases Findley dreams of executing involve the unfolding of human drama rather than the freezing of external reality: "I have visions of huge canvases . . . where there are masses of people in the picture . . . . They would be recordings of events. Or of moments" ("Alice" 11). Such a description recalls monumental canvases dealing with dramatic historical events such as Goya's *The Third of May, 1808* (1814–15), showing the shooting of Madrid resisters by Napoleon's troops, or Picasso's *Guernica* (1937), which depicts the bombing of a Basque town during the Spanish Civil War. Findley, noticing a reproduction of the latter painting during a conversation with David Macfarlane, appropriately focused on the striking movements of the wounded, rearing horse. "The love of life," Findley declared, "is in that rage" (6).

Many of Timothy Findley's characters, too, express this "love of life" through their actions and movements. Findley's fascination with gesture clearly derives from his work as a dancer and actor. In fact, Findley has explained that he embarked on an acting career after discovering that a fused disc made it impossible for him to dance professionally. Acting he regarded as an alternative means of attaining "the perfection of gesture" which one finds in dance (Macfarlane 5). More importantly, Findley frequently uses the metaphor of dance to describe the art of writing. "Dancing and writing are the same," he explained to David Macfarlane, "[i]t's a question of defining beauty within a gesture" (8). In a conversation with William Whitehead, Findley expanded on this analogy:

> What the dancer does is make a series of statements. And the statements are made up of gestures: gestures in a sequence. So words – words are the vocabulary of literate gesture. . . . Words in a sentence are a written gesture. ("Alice" 20–21)

This image: "gestures in a sequence," suggests film or drama rather than still photography and it is here that Findley's other vocations, as a playwright and screenwriter, are significant. Findley feels that his experience as a writer of plays and television drama for the CBC has enormously influenced his fiction. Referring to his compulsion to write copious stage directions for his plays, Findley remarks of his fictional stage directions: "I am always seeing what the people are doing, when I write: as well as hearing what they're saying. I see and hear in tandem." Most playwrights and novelists, Findley senses, only *hear* ("Alice" 12).

This desire to show as well as to tell his readers what is happening in the world of his characters has both enriched and occasionally marred his fiction. Novels such as *The Wars* and *Not Wanted on the Voyage* (1984) consist of a series of short scenes which are unified by interlocking patterns of vivid imagery, such as animal and fire imagery. These novels deserve the praise which Alberto Manguel recently bestowed on Findley's short fiction: "his stories are wonderfully visual, like plays acted out on the page at a breathtaking pace" (16). In a novel such as *The Butterfly Plague* (1969), however, a too-intrusive, less organized, and interlocking symbolism tends to direct the reader too much and in too many directions at once: butterflies, fire, jungles, beaches, disease, sun, and a mysterious figure who represents race are just a few examples of visual images in the work. Joan Coldwell's comment on the novel: "One is almost suffocated by significance" (258), could also read: "One is almost suffocated by visual images." In an interview with Donald Cameron in 1971, Findley confessed that he has a "fear of not having made a thing clear, and I'll write the same thing into a novel several times so that by the time I've got it said, I've said it eight different ways .... I don't trust enough – either myself or the reader" (54). This compulsion could be, in essence, the same compulsion which Findley felt as a playwright, to write frequent and detailed stage directions for his actors and actresses.

Findley's association of a series of gestures with his writing is especially evident when he describes the process of writing itself. For Findley, the first stage of writing – what the romantic writers would have termed "inspiration" – is a powerful visual experience. "Mind movies form the genesis of all my work," he once claimed at a conference on Canadian fiction and film. These "mind movies" consist of "a flow of images" running through the writer's mind, which, for Findley, are soon augmented by snatches of conversation ("The Novel as Film"). The difficult and frustrating task of the writer is, of course, to preserve these visual and aural fragments in the form of a permanent written record. "The perfect book," Findley told David Macfarlane, "goes by in a moment in your brain. And then you ask yourself, 'How in the name of God can I make that happen on a piece of paper?' " (6).

One method Findley uses is to fix upon what he calls one "persistent image" which resembles a photographic still shot ("The Novel as Film"). For example, Findley claims that the conversation between Robert Ross and his mother in the bathroom – one of the most vivid and perceptive scenes in *The Wars* – grew out of his fascination with the image of the drain-hole of the sink, into which Mrs. Ross's cigarette ashes "fall down the porcelain slopes like mountain climbers tumbling to their death" (23). This process resembles one described by Alice Munro, where her "persistent image" of a hermit coming down a hill forms the nucleus of the story "Images." Haunting images for Findley include those which he enumerates in his introduction to his short story collection *Dinner Along the Amazon* (1984): "The sound of screen doors banging," "Colt revolvers hidden in bureau drawers," "a chair that is always falling over," and, of course, "photographs in cardboard boxes" (ix). In addition, Findley says that his entire oeuvre grows out of one static, overwhelmingly "persistent image" – that of a cow and her calf standing in a white room, one of whose walls is smeared with blood, and the calf appears to be wondering: "Why are we here?" Findley confesses: "[t]hat is the overriding image of my life, that we are here for the slaughter" (Macfarlane 6).

More often, however, Findley describes himself as trying to record an ongoing process or conversation, working from a film clip rather than a snapshot. In "Alice Drops Her Cigarette on the Floor," Findley's lively conversation with William Whitehead, he compares himself to a voyeur who is eavesdropping on an argument between two fictional characters, George and Brenda, "when, all at once, Alice drops her cigarette on the floor .... so I make a record of it: ALICE DROPS HER CIGARETTE ON THE FLOOR" (13). This "record," interestingly, resembles a stage direction.

Frequently, Findley describes this visual experience as a visitation by one of his characters. "They arrive on your doorstep," he tells Donald Cameron, "and they say, I am coming into your life and I am not going to leave until I am down on the paper ... " (53). This method might be termed the "persistent character" approach. For two of his novels, Findley describes such visitations in detail:

> The first thing I see is the person, and the person will come and you'll hear this in your mind. (*knocking sound*); and you go to the door and you open the door and standing there is Hooker Winslow [from *The Last of the Crazy People*, 1967] with a cat in his arms. And he says: I'm in trouble, babble, babble, babble, and a scene evolves ... (Gibson 136)

Similarly, *The Wars* began, according to Findley, as an image of "a young man in a uniform, walking away from a military encampment, past a tent. In the tent was a letter in an opened letter case, and an uncapped pen" (Macfarlane 6). How appropriate it is that Findley's first image of Robert, a man who distinguishes himself through a courageous and unconventional act, should be an image of a young man in motion.

Although these visitations seem akin to the act of watching a film (where the viewer must coordinate sound and vision in order to assemble a meaning), Findley has explicitly compared them to photographic processes. "[i]t's like a developing picture in the pan," he explained to Johan Aitken, "that comes more and more into focus, and more and more into view. What you're seeing and hearing – yes everybody, photographs can be heard . . . " (80). One notes, nevertheless, that Findley chooses a metaphor of process and augments it by adding an imagined attribute – sound. Whether comparing the writing of novels to photography, dancing, painting, or to writing plays, Findley always emphasizes process and flux rather than fixity and stillness.

This preference is deeply embedded in Findley's notions of reality and realism and it affects the way in which he uses and views photography in his fiction. His emphasis on process – on the writer assimilating visual and aural stimuli from the external world – bespeaks a concern for subjectivity which differs enormously from Munro's concern with textures and surfaces. "Writers are never through with the world they see and hear," he writes in the introduction to *Dinner Along the Amazon*, "[e]ven in the silence of a darkened room, they see it and they hear it, because it is a world inside their heads, which is the 'real' world they write about" (xi). Even in another medium – paint, for instance – Findley's subjectivity overwhelms his desire to create documentary art: "And, when I sit down to paint, I inevitably paint something that is in my mind, rather than something out the window" ("Alice" 11). Whether in paint, words, or dance, Findley chooses to create – from "the silence of a darkened room" – his mind. One can therefore understand why the conflict between the photograph as lie and the individual's perception of the photograph as truth occupies such a prominent position in *Can You See Me Yet?*; it underlies not only the title question posed by Cassandra Wakelin to God, but much of Findley's thought.

"You begin . . . with photographs" (*The Wars* 5). The advice of the researcher-narrator of *The Wars* holds true for any student of Findley's use of visual images. "There were lots of photographs in our house," Findley recalls, "in boxes and albums. That was the period between 1895 and 1925 . . . . Everything was photographed, and so the whole of daily life was recorded by these photographs" (Aitken 82). As a matter of fact, Findley's analysis of the role of photography during those years is historically accurate. Photography historian Naomi Rosenblum, in her

World History of Photography (1984), observes that in the period from 1875 to 1925, "still another constituency was added to those who made and used camera images when ... simplified apparatus and processing methods – 'push button' photography – turned potentially everyone into a photographer" (245). Indeed, photographers such as Eugene Atget, Jacques-Henri Lartigue, and E. J. Bellocq (of whom we will hear more in our discussion of Michael Ondaatje) all undertook to photograph, in Findley's words, "the whole of daily life." Findley's comment, "I love the [photographs of] groups of people" (Aitken 82), again reveals his direct contact with the photography of the late nineteenth and early twentieth centuries; photographers of this period were fascinated by street scenes, showing groups of strolling people magically immobilized through the ever-faster speed of the camera shutter (Rosenblum, ch. 6). Both Rosenblum and Aaron Scharf (ch. 7) rightly associate this fascination with the impressionist painters' fascination with street scenes, evident in a work such as Monet's *Boulevard des Capucines* (1873 –74). One might even speculate that Findley's own desire to paint those "huge canvases ... where there are masses of people in the picture" ("Alice" 11) might well grow out of his fascination with those boxes of photographs he rummaged through as a child.

Although Findley attests to the photograph's power to reveal and to suggest movement or event, he also acknowledges its power to conceal and to fix: "Photographs are mysterious to me .... I still sit with a photograph and I think, if I could only get in there with you ... " (Aitken 83). Looking at the development of Findley's fiction from the earliest published stories to the most recent novels, one witnesses, in fact, Findley breaking down this barrier – no longer seeing the photograph as an external and artificial object but as a metaphor for the processes of memory and writing: as an image which beckons the author and reader alike to step into its frame.

Timothy Findley's early fiction is haunted by the figure of the sensitive, naïve young boy, who finds himself in the midst of a bizarre family crisis (whether war, alcoholism, insanity, or suicide) and who judges the situation entirely on the basis of what he sees. Often this complete absorption in literal detail (a camera-like perception) leads to a serious misinterpretation of the situation on the part of the child and, frequently, to an extreme act based on that misinterpretation.

In "Lemonade" from *Dinner Along the Amazon*, for instance (an early study for Findley's first novel, *The Last of the Crazy People*), Harper Dewey gradually discovers that the reason for his mother's sequestered existence is her alcoholism. Harper naïvely believes that removing the physical object which is causing his mother to withdraw her affection from him will solve the problem. He therefore sells his mother's gin, masked by the camouflaging agent of lemonade, to an increasingly tipsy neighbourhood, hoping to use the proceeds from the sale to repurchase the expensive jewellery which his mother has sold in order to support her habit.

Associated with this child-like state of illusion and the horrors of the revelations which progressively break in upon it, is the image of the photograph. After hearing a neighbour's loud complaints about the nocturnal carousings of his mother, Harper agitatedly bursts into his mother's room, where she is still sleeping, only to behold "[h]is mother's face pressed against the sheets ... a horrid yellowy white" like "a vile photograph forced before his eyes" (10). The photograph here is a pitiless revealer of harsh reality, reminiscent of the ruthless vision found in naturalistic novels such as Dreiser's *Sister Carrie* (1900) and Bennett's *The Old Wives' Tale* (1908). Like Harper, the camera is prepared to deal only with literal truth. One is again reminded of this relentless photographic vision when Harper's mother, Renalda, surveys the cosmetic mask which she has created in order to conceal the ravages of time and alcoholism:

> She looked into the mirror. It was as though she couldn't find herself there. She had to go very close to it

and lean one hand against the table to steady herself and she had to almost close her eyes before she found what she was looking for. (13)

Renalda's mirror is a type of camera analogue, for it faithfully reflects the mask, while concealing "what she was looking for" – her past self, the affectionate woman who once existed before the war and the loss of her young husband. Significantly, Renalda must almost close her eyes before she can recapture the memory of what once lay behind the mask.

One further aspect of this "vile photograph" which deserves mention is its resemblance, in Harper's mind, to "an advertisement for sickness" (10). This particular – commercial – use of photography, whether in advertising or film – always carries negative associations for Findley, as I shall discuss in more depth in relation to *The Butterfly Plague.*

Probably more influential in determining Findley's use of photography in "Lemonade" and in the rest of his early fiction is his negative feeling toward the past. When Harper visits the home of the neighbourhood "witch" Miss Kennedy, he notices "pictures on the wall of people who wore strangling, old costumes and who all looked as though life had been extremely painful for them. He concluded that they well might have been Miss Kennedy's 'victims.' Not one of them smiled" (18). The unsmiling countenances in these old family photographs are by no means unusual, for in the days of longer exposure times, subjects had to sit still for several minutes. (In the early days of the daguerreotype, they were often strapped in or placed in a vise.) Harper is, of course, seeing the lives of others through the distorting lens of his own bizarre life – a life which has indeed been an "extremely painful" one. In addition, Harper's perception of Miss Kennedy's family as "victims" is ironic and yet all too understandable, for in Harper's experience, family members do make victims of each other.

The link between victimization and the past is strongly forged not only in Harper Dewey's mind, but in Findley's mind as well. Harper sees the house in which he has been shut off from his mother, shut off from any knowledge of her problem, as "a house of the past" (38). We are also given a momentary glimpse of an older Harper Dewey's reluctance to visit in his memory this suffocating house of the past: "Perhaps he was turning from childhood – although he did not feel it going from him. His sense of loneliness was to determine this, beginning to become the loneliness of an adult, the loneliness defined by remembrance" (34). Here one senses Findley himself speaking through his narrator. He has mentioned in conversations with William Whitehead and Graeme Gibson details of his own lonely and painful childhood: the absence of his father during the war and his early contact with a woman "close to me who had to be placed in a mental institution" (Findley, "Alice" 17). Writing, then, may have been a way of dealing with that pain; Findley told Graeme Gibson that he began to write long novels one year during "that crucial adolescent period," when he was sick with a blood disease (124). Indeed, writing and loneliness are constant companions, according to Findley: "loneliness perverts, and this is very disturbing, very upsetting and you have to go through that to be a writer" (126–27).

In "War," another story from this early period, Findley once again confronts "the loneliness defined by remembrance." The narrator, Neil, a young boy whose father, like Findley's, left his family during the war, begins to confront this painful memory by confronting a photograph:

> That's my dad in the middle. We were just kids then, Bud on the right and me on the left. That was taken just before my dad went into the army.
> Some day that was. (*Dinner* 65)

The direct presentation of a photograph, as though the narrator were conducting the reader through a photograph album, as well as the suggestion that a story lies behind the inno-cent-seeming photograph, recalls an earlier tale of war which begins with a photograph, Ernest Hemingway's "Soldier's Home" from *In Our Time* (1925). After presenting a fraternity photograph of Krebs (an image of pre–war carelessness), Hemingway creates the following wry, photographic contrast:

> There is a picture which shows him on the Rhine with two German girls and another corporal. Krebs and the corporal look too big for their uniforms. The German girls are not beautiful. The Rhine does not show in the picture. (89)

The naïve conception of war as glamorous, as heightened tourism, is thus dealt a crushing blow. Similarly, in Findley's story, a seemingly innocent, even sentimental family portrait becomes, in effect, a type of domestic war photograph. Neil, discovering to his shock that his father has enlisted in the army, retreats to the hayloft, from where he throws stones at his father. (Harper Dewey, too, resorts to violence by throwing a stone through his mother's window, and Eugene Taffler in *The Wars* defines war as "one little David against another . . . Just a bunch of stone throwers" [33].) When Findley returns to the photograph at the end of the story, we, as readers, can now perceive the violent emotions which lie (like the Rhine in Hemingway's photograph) beyond the visual surface. The only vestiges of the domestic war which Neil has waged against his father are the resulting "war wounds" on his father's face – emblems of the psychological wounds which Neil must carry within him: "He looked just like he does right there in that picture. You can see where the stone hit him on his right cheek – and the one that knocked him out is the one over the eye" (81).

In creating this photograph of a family war, Findley has relied a great deal on the traditional iconography of war photography. Certain scenes and arrangements continually resurface in these horrible depictions of human misery, whether they date from the American Civil War, the First World War, or the Vietnam war – shots of grieving families, of atrocities in the very act of being committed, to name only two gruesome examples. In this story Findley echoes a frequent motif in war photography: that of two soldiers supporting a wounded fellow soldier. (Neil's "wounded" father, we recall, is flanked by his two sons.) Another recurring image in these photographs is that of the mother or father grieving over the body of a dead child. The fact that Neil is the soldier in this particular combat who sustains the deepest, most lasting wounds may reflect the truth which photographers of families plagued by war have often perceived; that war involves more than the movements of battalions, it strikes at the very heart of human life – the family.

The photograph plays an additional role in "War" – that of a talisman or symbol of an unforgettable past. Neil purchases two birch-bark boxes as presents for his mother and father, and in them he places objects which clearly represent his feelings towards his family. In his mother's box he places some pretty red stones which he has collected at the farm he has visited – the same *red* stones which he later fires at his father in anger. His original gift to his father – a golf ball – becomes, like the stones, a volatile missile rather than an affectionate present, and Neil therefore replaces it with a lasting reminder of his love and his bitterness: the photograph whose history and meaning we now know. Neil's closing remark, that "[t]here still is" a photograph lying in the box which he gave his father on the eve of his departure (81), projects us into Neil's future. One assumes that Neil's father has died in the war, and that the box and the photograph have returned (unlike the futile stones) to the sender. More importantly, the continued existence of the photograph in the box attests to the persistence of these damaging memories of the past; the picture in Neil's mind of his sense of betrayal, like the picture in the box, is a permanent fixture, a part of the ongoing war which one fights with oneself.

✦ *The Last of the Crazy People* (1967) ✦

Photography remains an eloquent reminder of the wars one fights with the past in Findley's first published novel, *The Last of the Crazy People*. Hooker Winslow, like his fictional ancestor Harper Dewey, possesses a camera-like sensitivity to the often confusing and contradictory stimuli offered by the external world. The very first sentence of the novel, "All night long, Hooker Winslow's eyes were open" (3), establishes him at once as the "seeing eye" of the novel, just as surely as Christopher Isherwood establishes one of his perceivers at the beginning of his *Berlin Diary* (1938): "I am a camera with its shutters open, quite passive, recording, not thinking .... Some day all this will have to be developed, carefully printed, fixed" (289). For Findley, the child, in particular, is a spotless, sensitive recording plate; as his character Cassandra in *Can You See Me Yet?* declares, "I never was an artful child. No fancies. Only what I saw" (84). Similarly, Juliet D'Orsey in *The Wars* humorously recalls her childhood role as "a born observer. Boswell in bows" (168). Again, one senses an autobiographical element at work, for of his own childhood experience with a mentally ill family member, Findley has said, "I was old enough to watch and listen and see what was happening and to make concise deductions and come to precise conclusions" ("Alice" 17-18).

Just as the camera may occasionally be said to lie, so too can the sensitive, perceiving child be led to wrong deductions and imprecise conclusions which are nevertheless based on a perceived reality. Like Harper Dewey, Hooker relies, in a child-like (and camera-like) fashion, on the literal. Caught eavesdropping on his father's vain pleas to his wife to come out of her room, Hooker stammers an explanation for his presence: "Going to the bathroom." Nicholas's wry rejoinder, "On the stairs?", completely escapes the frightened Hooker, who replies: "No sir. I mean I was going up to wash." Nicholas observes: "[r]eally . . . the child has no sense of humor" (37).

What Hooker lacks – especially in his terrified and nervous state – is not a sense of humour, but a sense of irony. Like most young children, he apprehends the literal first, and then only gradually the metaphorical or ironical. Hooker's brother Gilbert reflects, after hearing the maid Iris's oddly Ontarian version of the New Orleans ballad, "Frankie and Johnnie," that Hooker "would believe anything. He'd believe it if you told him that the world was going to end" (44). Later, Hooker ironically does believe that his world – his family – will be destroyed when he once again interprets an adult turn of phrase in a literal manner. Speaking to Nicholas about Gilbert's misbehaviour – his allegedly getting a neighbourhood girl pregnant – Aunt Rosetta explodes: " 'Shotgun! They're going to hold a shotgun over your son, and you just sit there!' . . . Hooker trembled. Shotgun?" (120). This misapprehension leads to Hooker's arming himself with the appropriately literal counterpart to Rosetta's metaphor: a gun.

Like Hooker, and like many of Alice Munro's characters, the other members of the Winslow family are characterized by the nature of their vision – or by their lack of it. Our first glimpse of Nicholas Winslow is one of a silent, weary man with "tired eyes" that "appeared to be fighting back the remaining images of a bad day" (33). If Hooker's problem is an oversensitivity to visual and aural messages, Nicholas's is surely an unwillingness to confront what he perceives. His mentally disturbed wife (whose mental disturbance largely stems from his forcing children on her) is shut away from his sight, like Rochester's hapless wife in *Jane Eyre*. Nicholas also refuses to see the signs of restlessness and despair in his son Gilbert, who can only capture the attention of his father by staging a horrifying spectacle: his suicide. Gilbert himself is a recorder of images and feelings, yet he too locks himself up – in the study. Like Del Jordan in *Lives of Girls and Women*, he is a maker of lists:

> endless lists. Lists of dates and lists of places. Lists of hockey stars, movie stars, historical figures. Lists of battles, generals, victories. Lists of poets, playwrights, authors. Lists of occasions, real and imaginary – occasions such as birthdays, anniversaries, public holidays. Timetables. (259)

On the rare occasions when Hooker visits the study, Gilbert has him recite the titles of the leather-bound books on the shelf. All of these lists, however, remain hidden and futile; Gilbert can never record – and thus rid himself of – the pain associated with his mother's illness. Unlike a later documentary writer in Findley's fictional world, Hugh Selwyn Mauberley in *Famous Last Words* (1981), Gilbert never does sort out and communicate his vision and his pain.

Not only are the Winslows the victims of crippled vision, they also curb Hooker's vision. "Don't stand right there, honey, in the doorway," cries Iris to Hooker, who is excitedly awaiting a glimpse of his mother on the day of her return from the hospital. "Stand back outa the way" (12). Hooker's family is continually placing him on the periphery, shooing him out to play, hiding the facts of his mother's illness or of Gilbert's troubles from him – in short, impairing his vision.

This curtailing of vision is associated by Findley with a stultifying fixity or lack of movement. Hooker's staring into the black night, at the beginning of the novel, is emblematic of his condition: that of the sensitive perceiver who is deprived of objects to see and comprehend. Even his nightmares, we are told, like those of his cat, always end "with a wakened stare" (4). The entire prologue, which shows Hooker's early morning journey from the house to the stable, from where he will later shoot his parents, is pervaded by this sense of fixity: "Across the yard it remained quiet, and there was a moment that was utterly static" (8). Looking deeply into his cat's eyes, he sees them as "spheres of innocence and age" (9), just as his own eyes are those of a child who has, ironically, perceived a great deal, and who has yet been denied knowledge or vision. The prologue itself becomes a still-shot – a still moment before the purging of Hooker's bitterness and pain: "Now, the boy and the cat waited and were still" (9).

Hooker's terrifying still moment of insanity, we learn, is the final result of the fixity and stagnation which have surrounded the entire Winslow household. Hooker continually sees his family as lifeless, frozen icons; when Jessie returns from the hospital, for instance, the neglected Hooker perceives that "As people, they solidified . . . and they became the absolutes of all the little things that once they had only partly been. They 'froze,' as Hooker said" (12). While Aunt Rosetta and Gilbert engage in a passionate argument about Gilbert's "scandalous" behaviour, Hooker can only try to lip-read their words, only to find that "it was impossible. Rosetta was completely frozen" (224). Rosetta, a wraith-like figure of death-in-life, is physically frozen as well; a stroke has rendered one side of her face entirely immobile.

The family's physical stasis is only the outer manifestation of a hopeless inner stagnation. Nicholas realizes the full extent of this passivity when he confesses after Gilbert's death, "I can't do anything, when something's wrong like this . . . I can't even move" (250). This inability to respond to each other has indeed been the plague which has destroyed the family. As Rosetta herself realizes much earlier in the novel, the mental disturbances of Jessie and Gilbert are not the causes of the family's passivity, but its consequences: "I think we let them get sick . . . Because of always being afraid. To *do* anything" (62). Rosetta's remark remains unheeded, however, even when it is borne out by the death of Gilbert. The true and all-encompassing symbol of this decaying family – the image which broods over the entire novel – is Jessie Winslow's stillborn baby.

Not surprisingly, photography in *The Last of the Crazy People* becomes an emblem of unnatural fixity. Iris recreates for her friend Alberta the nightmarish life of the Winslow family: "These people are all asleep . . . Day and night. They lock themselves up in a bunch of old rooms. They make their whole life round things that are dead . . . In that Rosetta's office there's nothin' but pictures of old dead people" (92). Later in the novel, when Hooker confronts these family photographs, he senses the enormous gulf between his own family and the figures in the photographs, "balanced on the edge of eternity forever, smiling and poised and dead" (253). Although Hooker recognizes the town in the photograph to be the same town which he inhabits, the denizens of the photographic world appear to him as silent, frozen creatures bearing no real connection to the world which Hooker knows: "None of them spoke. Not one of them looked directly into the lens of the camera. He perceived that they were quiet and different. They seemed contented, pleased" (255). Only in the photograph of Grandfather Winslow do we perceive that the pain experienced by the present Winslows has not been entirely unknown to their neatly preserved ancestors. Unlike the meek creatures of the other photographs, Grandfather Winslow faces the camera (a sign of revelation), thus allowing us to penetrate beyond the fixed mask of his puritan ethics: "He was trying, it seemed, very hard to impress on posterity the fact that life for him was something strict and moral. Yet, in his eyes, he failed to do so. There was something to witness otherwise, for they attested to the pain of life" (254).

Hooker's family has followed in the footsteps of Grandfather Winslow, in creating a fixed mask to cover their pain and vulnerability. As Hooker scans the family photographs, he repeatedly glimpses Aunt Rosetta's "round, worried stare" (the same image of fixed vision which we have seen associated with Hooker). Hooker senses Rosetta's "sad aloofness" in one photograph and is even sensitive enough to understand that "[s]he just wanted to be safe, and that meant cold and sure and true and touchless" – like her stilted photographs (257). Even her opinions share the lifelessness of her photographs; they "had been firmly decided, long ago, some time in the olden days, the day before her photographs" (257). Hooker and his family, in their profound alienation from the past, resemble those characters in Chekhov who, according to Findley, "are transfixed, unable to move with any kind of joy into the past and, thus, unable to conjure any sense of the future at all" ("The Countries of Invention" 106).

Hooker's final inability to "conjure any sense of the future" leads him to violence and murder – acts which are also strongly associated with photography. His misreading of the town photograph, like his literal acceptance of Alberta's fundamentalist welcoming of Armageddon as the end of suffering, leads

Figure 1

Diane Arbus, *A Family on Their Lawn One*
Sunday in Westchester, N.Y. (1968)
[Estate of Diane Arbus]

Figure 2

Walker Evans, *Boots,* from *Let Us
Now Praise Famous Men* (1941)
[Estate of Walter Evans]

Figure 3

Joseph Devellano, *Telephoto*, (1982)
[Art Gallery of Hamilton]

Figure 4

Anonymous, *Les abords du crematoire
à la liberation en 1945, Dachau*

Figure 5

from *Running in the Family*
[Permission of Michael Ondaatje]

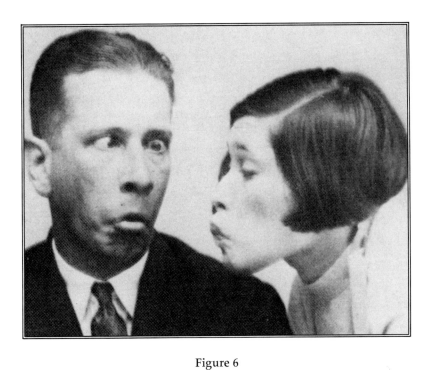

Figure 6

What We Think of Married Life,
from *Running in the Family*
[Permission of Michael Ondaatje]

him to conceive of death as a type of suspended state of happiness – a comforting still-shot. Ironically, then, Hooker resorts to a "shot" at the end of the novel to put an end to the pain which he and his family have experienced.

The photograph has been christened the "guillotining of the moment" by A.D. Coleman (133), and this link between photography and violence is repeatedly emphasized in *The Last of the Crazy People*. Hooker relives, at one point, the famous camera image of Jack Ruby shooting Lee Harvey Oswald and is impressed by Gilbert's opinion that Oswald killed in order to gain "[h]appiness" (69). After Gilbert's death, Hooker is seized by the memory of yet another violent image – the photograph of "a naked man lying dead in the ruins of a fire" (264). Even in the seemingly idyllic photographs of his ancestors, there lies a hidden, menacing undercurrent; they are frequently taken near sundown or "toward the dark side of the evening" and the encroaching shadows are "long and menacing." Even the brightly clothed children in the photographs "looked like dusty moths, hovering, yet stilled, forever, at the edge of the dark" (256).

This suggestion of mortality inherent in the photograph, especially when viewed by a young child, is not infrequent in literature. One thinks, for instance, of Katherine Anne Porter's "Old Mortality," which opens with two young girls' awed perceptions of their late aunt's photograph: "a motionless image in her dark walnut frame . . . a ghost in a frame" (3-4). Such uses of photography would not be unfamiliar to Findley, who shares with Alice Munro a liking for American writers of the South, such as Carson McCullers (Gibson 138).

The most vivid symbol of the association between photography and mortality in this novel is the photograph of the dead serviceman, John Harris. Harris, eighteen years of age at the time of the photograph, is the epitome of childhood innocence; he is "sweet-eyed," with "large and luminous eyes." Nevertheless, Hooker's (and our) awareness of his death in the war forces us to perceive a grim posthumous irony in the photograph: "the expression on his face was that of someone who could only remember something sad" (96). After Gilbert's death, the image of John Harris becomes one more of what H. J. Rosengarten calls "the jumbled images" of death which run through Hooker's mind (79). Moreover, the Winslows own a twin photograph of John Harris – a sign of their continuing alliance with death – and Rosetta even addresses the still photograph at a particularly crucial moment in the family's disintegration: " 'Family,' she said to John Harris. 'It's come to be the worst word I know, now.' John Harris smiled." At this moment, Jessica Winslow's voice breaks in upon Rosetta's colloquy with the dead boy, providing an unwittingly mordant commentary: "Dead . . . dead . . . dead . . . " (153).

Photography and death are, as we have discovered in the preceding chapter, traditional companions, but in Findley photography itself is seen as an aggressive act analogous to murder – a concept which is entirely absent in Alice Munro's fiction. The camera and the gun are equally destructive weapons in *The Last of the Crazy People*. When Hooker discovers the photograph of John Harris, he also discovers, lying at its side in a wooden box, a gun – the gun which he eventually uses to allow his parents to enter the blessed oblivion of the photographed people. In a richly suggestive scene, Findley describes the young Hooker turning "in a slow arc, sighting various gloomy chairs, and then, pulling until the hammer clicked, he took a shot at the photograph of John Harris" (97).

The link between gun and camera has, in fact, been noted by various writers, artists, and critics of photography. Susan Sontag, quoting camera advertisements which read like promotions for a Webley, asserts that "there is something predatory in the act of taking a picture . . . . Just as the camera is a sublimation of the gun, to photograph someone is a sublimated murder – a soft murder, appropriate to a sad, frightened time" (*On Photography* 14–15). Jorge Lewinski, writing about the motivation of war photographers, sardonically asks:

is the camera not a substitute for a gun? . . . On the one hand, he [the war photographer] is able to experience the supreme stimulation of the war adventure, with its attendant dangers; on the other hand, he has the opportunity to perform a seemingly noble deed – to fight the evil and outrage of war by depicting its horror in his photographs. Who could ask for more? (13)

Photographers themselves have become uneasily aware of this implication; many object to the expression, "taking a picture," and have amended it to suggest a more positive creative act: "making a picture." Painters, too, have seized upon this revealing contemporary analogy; in a recent show of Canadian painter Joseph Devellano's works at the Hamilton Art Gallery, two canvases were placed side by side – one showing a young man aiming a camera at the viewer (see fig. 3), the other showing the same young man aiming a rifle.

This equation of the gun and the camera sums up Findley's early attitude toward photography. The "violent stillness" (279) which envelops Nicholas Winslow when his son pulls the trigger is not only a metaphor for the psychological state of the Winslow family. For Timothy Findley, photography itself is "violent stillness."

✦ *The Butterfly Plague* (1969) ✦

Findley's second novel appears to be a radical departure from his very earliest fiction, moving from the Ontarian family to the terrifyingly parallel worlds of Nazi Germany and Hollywood during the 1930s, from autobiography and close psychological scrutiny to social and ideological criticism. Nevertheless, Findley has explicitly warned readers against making "the mistake ... of thinking that because it became larger, it didn't home in on families too." The Damarosch family, with their phobic consciousness of the curse on their blood – haemophilia – are "very like the Winslows," according to Findley (Gibson 139). As one might expect, photography occupies some of the roles which it did in the earlier fiction: that of a metaphor for fixity and violence, for example. In *The Butterfly Plague*, however, these associations in Findley's mind appear even more intense; photography comes to represent a type of spiritual fascism in the decadent Hollywood society. In addition, photography, for the first time in Findley's works, is explicitly associated with artificiality and lies, largely because of its relationship to film and thus to the entire aura of glamour and falsehood surrounding Hollywood.

For the first time as well, Findley adopts some of the techniques of the documentary film-writer or photographer.

The entire novel takes the form of a journal, with entries identified not only by day, month, and year, but also by location and hour. Unlike *The Last of the Crazy People*, where Hooker serves as a perceptive though limited "camera eye," here a third-person narrator assumes photographic omniscience. In fact, he introduces himself to the reader as a "chronicler of history" as opposed to a "writer of fiction" (272). This chronicler, unlike Hooker Winslow, can see beyond visual surfaces; at one point, for instance, he records "A silent, unseen reaction" (53) on the part of the aging star, Letitia Virden. Gradually, one senses the air of documentary veracity being undermined by fantasy, by the hoards of monarch butterflies which flock to California, or by the bizarre fire in the Alvarez Canyon which Ruth Damarosch later discovers that she has imagined.

This mixture of documentary and fantasy – again, magic realism – is entirely appropriate to a work which deals with the truth and lies of modern experience. Photography is conceived to be a purveyor of lies – not because it reveals what is not present, but because it only reveals what is physically apparent. Letitia Virden, who wishes to make a Hollywood "comeback" at an advanced age, is one of the chief dealers in photographic lies. When the "Hollywood News Vignettes" camera, covering Letitia's reentry into Hollywood life, approaches her too closely, she "suddenly turned away and placed a veil over her face" (193), in order to dupe the supposed all-seeing eye. When Letitia finally does make a new film, "[p]hotographed through tinted gauze" (332), she rages at the appearance on film of a microscopic mole on her neck. Findley's narrator explicitly relates this rage for superficial perfection, for the photographic lie, to fascism:

> *Madonna ha sempre ragione.*
> Mussolini is always right.

> (332)

Even at the end of *The Butterfly Plague*, after Ruth Damarosch has rejected this false ideal of perfection, Letitia Virden and the photographic lie live on; Ruth sees in the newspapers "photos of Letitia" which "had been outrageously retouched. She looked like something carved in marble" – a supreme image of artificiality and of fixity (354). Findley would doubtless agree with Susan Sontag, that "fascism ... stands for an ideal or rather ideals that are persistent today under the other banners: the ideal of life as art, the cult of beauty ..." ("Fascinating Fascism" 319).

Other characters in *The Butterfly Plague* destroy themselves because they cannot compete with this photographic perfection. The voluptuous though vacuous starlet Myra panics when she realizes that she is becoming older (thirty-two) and less able to match the popular photographic image of herself; she abuses her body by lying about and consuming untold amounts of chocolates. As Dolly Damarosch wryly reflects after Myra's suicide: "You die when you can't be real .... When you can't see who you are and when you cannot see what is" (303). Photography impedes our vision of these things by imposing upon the flux of our lives a static, rigid ideal belonging to the past.

Dolly himself is so emotionally crippled by his physical "flaw" – his haemophilia – that he assembles a photographic gallery of perfect female bodies to act as a substitute for developing a close human relationship. When Ruth enters his "antiseptic," "bloodless" apartment after his death, she sees, first of all, these public icons of perfection which Hollywood promotes: "From all around her the photograph eyes of film stars stared .... Glossy eyes, pretending to smile, pretending to brood, pretending to hypnotize, pretending to live" (321). This pretense, however, like Dolly's life, only serves to conceal a more pathetic reality; when Ruth picks some of Dolly's child-hood books off the shelf, she discovers, lodged between their pages, Dolly's private photograph album: explicit photographs of homosexual acts. As in the fascist ideology, Findley suggests, the rage for perfection here produces not perfection but frustration. As Ruth sadly observes, not even these private photographs of Dolly's inner desires are free of glaring artifice:

The faces of the models ... seemed like the faces of automatons. Their eyes held no expression whatsoever. Occasionally, one appeared to be smiling, but, studied more closely, it could be seen that the smile was superimposed, not conjured the way an actor might conjure an expression contrary to his own emotion, but literally laid on, as though, just before the photo was taken, the photographer had rearranged the facial features with his fingers .... Life was a posture, forever. (326)

Ruth refers to these clumsily arranged figures as the "paper people" (329), providing a link with another work of Findley's which sheds light on the question of artifice and truth in *The Butterfly Plague*: his CBC play, *The Paper People* (1967). It, too, is a reworking of the documentary form, for it appears to be a documentary about a researcher making a documentary about an artist named James Reid Taylor. One of Taylor's art forms is the burying of personal friends in layers of *papier mâché*, so as to form a shell or doll, which he then burns. These paper people, like those of Dolly Damarosch, are symbols of a perverted art form, in which artifice becomes no more than a hollow, futile sham.

Unlike James Reid Taylor's ritualistic "people" burnings, Ruth's burning of both sets of Dolly's paper people is not a futile or violent act, but an attempt to cleanse and purge the world of the photographic lie and its underlying perversion. In addition, her last glimpse of the apartment, before she sets it on fire, is of the family photographs which stare back at her mockingly. "All these faces, the faces, too, inside the books" (327) merge in Ruth's mind, suggesting that not only Hollywood, but also the drive for perfection within the Damarosch family – especially within George Damarosch, who "glared" from his photograph – have been responsible for the lie of Dolly's life.

Ironically, the visionaries in *The Butterfly Plague* are not always those who see, in photographic fashion, what is there; they are sometimes those who see what is *not* there. Findley has called Naomi Nola Damarosch "a realist in every sense" (Gibson 147), for she, unlike Myra and Letitia, is able to relinquish the photographic vision of herself as a young actress, never growing old. Pain, too, she accepts, both in deciding to have children in spite of her haemophilia, and in her stoic acceptance of approaching death. Indeed, when she dies, the neighbourhood child who finds her body appropriately remarks: "It was wrong, somehow, to close her eyes" (269). Nevertheless, Findley acknowledges the existence of another form of realism – a subjective or imaginative realism. Ruth

Damarosch, at one point in the novel, despairingly asks herself: "Is everything only in my mind?" (324). Her apocalyptic vision of the fire in Alvarez Canyon, in which a host of living creatures are trapped and destroyed, her mating with a horrifying machine-like member of a "Master Race," are all imaginary. Yet as Findley has explained, Ruth is not merely hallucinating, but imaginatively transforming the actual events of her day, such as the burning of the synagogues in Germany. "In fact," Findley insists, "her translation of reality was correct. An 'idea' was going around killing things. The idea of Fascism" (Gibson 146). Ruth's vision is thus opposed to the narrowly perfectionist and photographic vision of her day and is even different from Naomi's acceptance of "things as they are"; it is closer, instead, to what Findley once called "that large reality, which you define in books symbolically" (Gibson 147).

As in *The Last of the Crazy People*, photography is continually linked with violence. A disoriented Ruth, arriving at the Culver City station after her harrowing experiences in Germany, is immediately subjected to the prying eye of the camera. As her underwear spills out of her suitcase onto the ground, a photographer seizes on this chance to make the private public (24). Photography has meant indignity and unwanted revelation earlier in Ruth's life, when her Nazi husband, obsessed with her potential for physical perfection, published her picture – head shaved, clad in a uniform, like an inmate from a concentration camp (37). It is difficult to read these descriptions of Ruth's mistreatment without calling to mind the photographs taken at Dachau and Belsen.

Whereas in *The Last of the Crazy People* the photograph becomes equivalent to a gun, in *The Butterfly Plague* the destructive weapon is primarily the movie camera. George Damarosch, telling Ruth of the industrialist Cooper Carter who has taken over the production of Letitia Virden's film, describes him as a maker of "weapons": "Guns, tanks, bombs .... Sometimes ... movies" (202). Two of the death scenes in the novel, moreover, take the form of moving pictures: Naomi relives scenes and lines of dialogue from her films, and Dolly, racing down the highway towards his death, receives a series of impressions – "[p]ictures of death" (305). The witness of the accident, Octavius Rivi, the secret son of Letitia Virden and a reclusive movie watcher, cannot even recognize an off-screen death:

"Having seen so many films in his life, Octavius was only aware of the semblance of death. He did not know that, in real life, blood was a signal for absolute panic and concern" (314). This power of photography and film to distance us from felt experience has fascinated and distressed critics such as Susan Sontag, who argues that "[i]nsofar as photography does peel away the dry wrappers of habitual seeing, it creates another habit of seeing: both intense and cool, solicitous and detached . . . " (*On Photography* 99).

One senses the same fear of the camera as a dehumanizing tool in *The Butterfly Plague*. Sontag's uneasiness is based on her perception of the photograph as an artificial freezing of the continuum of our lives which reduces its ability to convey truth and, of course, increases its ability to lie. In "Fascinating Fascism" from *Under the Sign of Saturn*, she explicitly condemns the photographs of former Nazi film director Leni Riefenstahl for this dehumanization, this turning of "people into things" and "preoccupation with situations of control" (316). In the scene of the burning of Alvarez Canyon, Findley captures precisely the same associations between fascism and fixity:

> The chains of the fence bulged; almost gave – but did not. Paws reached through. Beggars peered. Dead. Noses, eyes, portions of torn and unrecognizable anatomy dropped before Ruth, melting in the grass at her feet. She turned back. It was over. No more noises. Four thousand creatures had perished against a wall. (143)

Again, one is reminded of Jamie Taylor's burning *papier mâché* bodies in *The Paper People* and even more powerfully of the victims of the gas ovens in the German concentration camps. All of these obsessions – fixity, fascism, and photography – will return, like ominous hoards of monarch butterflies, twelve years later in *Famous Last Words*.

The stories which Findley wrote in the mid-1970s reveal both a continuation of and a divergence from his fictional use of the photograph in earlier works. As in virtually all of his fiction, Findley stresses the act of seeing; in "What Mrs. Felton Knew," an apocalyptic tale of a large-scale plan to eliminate rural dwellers, vision remains one of the enduring, indestructible human traits. Barney Lambert, one of the remaining "Rural Expendables" in this Orwellian tale, resorts to a final survival tactic: "He was going to do what perhaps no one else had done till now. He was going to force a pair of eyes to look into his own. Someone had to *see* someone" (*Dinner* 129). All that Barney desires, before he is enveloped by the exterminating spray, is a "moment of recognition . . . a look to mark his own existence in another man's eyes . . ." (130). When he does achieve this meeting of eyes, however, he discovers not human contact, but a cold, automaton-like registering in the eyes of the sixteen-year-old exterminator.

In these stories of the seventies, Findley begins to use vision – especially this momentary vision which resembles a photographic still-shot – as a structural device. "The People on the Shore" begins and ends with the narrator's description of "a look of recognition and farewell" bestowed upon him when he was a child by a fellow hotel guest, Mrs. Lewis, before she dies (*Dinner* 133; 148). This refocusing technique allows the reader to read the information gained in the story into the still-shot at the end – a device which Findley uses with even greater skill in *The Wars*.

These stories also testify to Findley's continuing obsession with fixity and artificiality. In "Sometime – Later – Not Now," Diana, the ambitious pianist who discovers that she has fallen in love with a homosexual, is enveloped by psychological and artistic paralysis as a result. *"Miss Galbraith was one of those electrical machines that immobilizes things at the touch"* (*Dinner* 107), complains one music critic, and the narrator observes of an older and bitterer Diana, "The tone – the pitch – the gaze remained the same. Fixed" (109). In another story, "The Book of Pins," Findley once again uses the repeated image device as in "The People on the Shore," to recreate the stagnant atmosphere surrounding the writer, Annie Bogan. "The people were changed, perhaps," observes the narrator in the hotel lobby at the beginning and end of the story, "but never their image – [in the mirrors] never the basic reflection of what was there" (*Dinner* 204; 217). This static photographic image is entirely appropriate to a story dealing with the "pinning" down or victimizing of human beings.

In "Sometime – Later – Not Now" and "Hello Cheeverland, Goodbye," photographs once more become the symbols of an artificial mentality as in *The Butterfly Plague*. In the former story, Jean-Paul, who involves Diana's lover in a homosexual affair, uses "photographs of Nijinsky, Lincoln Kirsten and Josephine Baker" to construct a snobbish "cult of Paris" among his young male friends (*Dinner* 102). In "Hello Cheeverland, Goodbye," Ishmael, the naïve visitor to a nightmarish suburbia, is forced to face his own hollowness and degradation when a woman covers all of his walls with "a paper whorehouse" – explicit pictures from men's magazines (*Dinner* 186). This collage of cheap artificiality is, in fact, a fitting metaphor for Cheeverland itself.

The most remarkable development during these years of Findley's career is the photographic style which accounts for much of the powerful impact of *The Wars*. Short, staccato sentences allow Findley to accumulate visual details, as though he were actually describing a photograph or a filmed gesture: "She stands like a boy in my memory, wearing khaki shorts. Feet wide apart. Canvas running shoes" (*Dinner* 96). The short story itself becomes, like the photograph, an abrupt break in the flow of time, instead of a set piece with a formal introduction, body, and resounding conclusion. "[T]here are no beginnings, not even to stories," Findley begins "Losers, Finders, Strangers at the Door," there are "only places where you make an entrance into someone else's life and either stay or turn and go away" (*Dinner* 189). How remarkable it is that Findley's sentiments echo those of another intensely photographic short-story writer, Alice Munro:

> I can start reading them [short stories] anywhere; from beginning to end, from end to beginning, from any point in between in either direction. So obviously I don't take up a story and follow it as if it were a road, taking me somewhere, with views and neat diversions

along the way. I go into it, and move back and forth and settle here and there, and stay in it for a while. ("What is Real?" 224)

Entering a Findley story is like entering a fiction in Alice Munro's fashion; "We always arrive too late or too early in Timothy Findley's stories,"observes Alberto Manguel of *Dinner Along the Amazon*, "The event has already taken place, or will take place sometime later, once we have left the page, or perhaps it will never take place" (13). In the same way a viewer enters the world of the photograph, intensely aware that it represents only one drop in an immense pool of time, like the split-second image of a man jumping over a sidewalk puddle in a famous Cartier-Bresson photograph.

Findley's growing awareness of this suspended quality of certain moments in our existence accompanies an increasing value for the past and for human memory. In "The People on the Shore," Mrs. Lewis describes to the young Tiffy her dream of the hotel's inhabitants – past, present, and future – all standing on the shore, looking out to sea. In this dream-like telescoping of time, people whom Tiffy *"would* remember" join those mysterious beings out of the pages of the hotel's photo-graph album "in their photograph-clothes" (138) and Tiffy himself, "very, *very* old" (139). Mrs. Lewis's vision is therefore a vision of the continuity of human hopes and desires, from the far distant past into a future which is as misty and elusive as the sea. Memory itself becomes, for an older Tiffy, analogous to a photograph album – to a "sequence of rapidly fluttering photographs that tell a story in a few, quick seconds" (145). One could think of no better description of Findley's next major work, *The Wars*.

✦ *The Wars* (1977) ✦

Findley's *The Wars* is much more than an international best-seller, and, to quote Eric Thompson, "one of the most remark-able novels of war ever published" (99). It marks Findley's full recognition of the deep affinity between the photograph and memory, the past, and even the act of writing itself. The photograph becomes not only a major image (as it is in *The Last*

77

of the Crazy People) but the main structuring principle of the novel and the source of Findley's terse and strikingly visual style. It is no wonder that Findley's final note of acknowledgement preceding *The Wars* is directed to "M" for "the letters from which the photographs fell." "M" is Marian Engel, another consciously photographic writer, who corresponded with Findley while he was writing *The Wars* and who sent him photographs which, according to Findley, "gave whole passages of the book" ("The Tea Party" 38). Findley's own interest in photography was growing at the time as well; in 1976 he saw the first production of his play *Can You See Me Yet?* In retrospect, Findley has commented that "maybe the photographs in Cass's [Cassandra Wakelin's] album may have been the basis for the photographic technique of *The Wars*" ("Alice" 15).

In addition, the predominance of the photograph is entirely appropriate to a novel of the First World War – the first major war after the American Civil War in which photography actively shaped the impressions and opinions of those at home. As Laurie Ricou writes in a discussion of Findley and violence, leafing through the photographs in the *Illustrated London News* was a common occupation of wartime families. "Photographs," claims Ricou, "were the medium which conveyed news of the Great War with the greatest impact. They might well be said to be the art form of the Great War, the chief means of remembering that war, as film might be the art form of the second world war" (132). Findley's own experience of growing up during the latter war tends to confirm Ricou's statement; as Joan Coldwell notes, he was "[g]reatly affected as a child by newsreels of the Second World War . . ." (257). Speaking of his research for *The Wars*, however, Findley acknowledges two sources of information about the First World War: his soldier-uncle's letters which provided him with "documentary" details about the trenches, and photographs which "have been a great help to me in writing" (Aitken 83).

In *The Wars*, photographs become important analogues not only to the act of writing, but to the act of reading as well. As in *The Last of the Crazy People*, the prologue plunges us into the middle of a chronicle in which we, as readers, must move backward and forward. Juxtaposed with this isolated fragment from the story of Robert Ross's life – a glimpse of Robert and the horses after his desertion from the army – is another "beginning" of the novel: the researcher's beginning "at the archives with photographs."

Our first impression of this research is of the difficulties and frustration faced by the researcher – witnesses refusing to speak, the crumbling of delicate photographs. Only occasionally "the corner of a picture will reveal the whole" (5). All of these details provide a background for our own demanding research into the mysteries of Robert Ross's life – reading the novel. Like the researcher, we are presented with a "corner of a picture" – Robert Ross and the horses – from which we must deduce the whole – that is, the reason for Robert's act. Reading the segments or fictional "photographs" of *The Wars* which deal with Robert's family, his experiences with men and women, his first acquaintance with death, allows us to perceive what Juliet D'Orsey calls "the circles – all drawing inward to the thing that Robert did" (114).

The opening of *The Wars* is only one example of the way in which photography informs the very structure and style of the novel. Findley has constructed a novel made up entirely of short segments: thirty small scenes in part one dealing with Robert's experiences before leaving for the wars; thirteen segments depicting his first shocking experiences of the trenches; a journal-style account of one day (itself broken into segments according to the hour, to suggest the painful slowness of time when under siege); part four, a fragment of Lady Juliet D'Orsey's taped memories of Robert, occasionally interrupted by the now-aged Juliet's comments; and finally, fourteen segments narrating Robert's reentry into France and his desertion, all enclosed in a prologue and epilogue. Findley himself has repeatedly emphasized that this fragmented structure is, in fact, photographic. "*The Wars*," he commented to William Whitehead, "unfolds as a series of pictures" ("Alice" 16), and more recently he has likened the novel to a long avenue flanked at regular intervals by imposing billboards: "Flashing on these billboards are the selected photographs, the images, that I wanted to imprint of moments from the war, moments from Robert's life, moments from history . . . " (Aitken 84).

This desire to create a series of flashing, unforgettable photographs again reveals the close affinity between Findley's work as a dramatist and his development as a novelist. *Can You*

See Me Yet? is, like *The Wars*, a fast-paced series of short visual scenes. Indeed, Findley's justification of its photograph-like structure clearly echoes his billboard analogy: "In asylums – time flashes on and off, and in between the flashes, there's nothing: greyness, stillness, silence. Waiting. But the things that are seen in the flashes are astonishing. Riveting: vivid and stark ..." ("Alice" 15). Like the blinding flash of the camera, the dramatist's pacing and use of striking gestures freeze and illuminate a portion of human experience.

Even in the structure of individual paragraphs and sentences in *The Wars*, one senses these blinding flashes of illumination:

> He lifted his gaze to the rim.
> Nothing.
> He angled his head to the left.
> The bird sang.
> Robert froze.
> There was a German soldier with a pair of binoculars staring right at him. (146)

John Hulcoop has written extensively on the photographic nature of Findley's style, arguing that the "abbreviated paragraphs ... isolate actions, events, thoughts, emotions, images, or whatever Findley wants to focus on ..." ("Look! Listen!" 41). In this sense, fixity or stillness is a positive virtue in Findley's art, for it involves the capturing of recalcitrant experience which only the writer can effect.

Not all critics, however, perceive this pointillist style as a successful reminder of the workings of memory and the artistic imagination. John Moss, in *A Reader's Guide to the Canadian Novel*, sees Findley's style as an irritatingly neurological account of "a sequence of responses" (75-76). Michael Taylor, too, in a review of *The Wars*, denounces Findley's style as "a parody of the and-now-you-are-there approach of historical journalism ..." (173). Findley is, it is true, using such a photo-journalistic convention; he does want us to be "there" in the muddy trenches with Robert, and yet he is also turning the convention inside out, by admitting on occasion the difficulty faced by the researcher or photographer in creating a true picture of the wars: "There is no good picture of this except the one you can make in your mind ... " (77) and "the mud. There are no good similies" (78).

Eva-Marie Kröller, on the other hand, although she is intensely aware of the impact of photography on Findley's style and thought, tends to err in the opposite direction. Every dark room which Robert enters (the room at Desolé in which he is raped, for instance) is a potential *camera obscura* image, while even "the prostitutes [of Lousetown, Alberta] have become transparent" because of their transparent clothing, "threatening to emerge as a sickening new image like negatives in a developing tray" (70).

As these stylistic comments indicate, Kröller sees photography in *The Wars* as an image suggesting threatening enclosure. She argues that "Findley's interpretation of photography as isolating man from his natural context and turning him into a two-dimensional grid, as well as giving man the power to do the same to his environment, rank it together with all other surveying strategies as one of the weapons of earth against world ..." (72). Yet I would argue that photography in *The Wars* becomes humanity's weapon against the loss of the all-important memory – the memory of the misery and futility of the wars.

Findley uses photography in *The Wars* to underline one of the most important ideas in the novel: the necessary interpenetration of the public and the private in any complete understanding of a war. "What you have to accept at the outset is this," insists Findley's narrator, "many men have died like Robert Ross, obscured by violence" (5). Private violence serves to enlarge in our minds the overwhelming horror of the 1914–18 carnage. "So far," we are told near the end of the novel, "you have read of the deaths of 557,017 people – one of whom was killed by a street-car, one of whom died of bronchitis and one of whom died in a barn with her rabbits" (185).

The series of photographs which the researcher surveys at the beginning of *The Wars* reveals this same modulation from public to private fact. At first, the photographs function as mirrors of the age – revealing changing fashions, entertainments, and the growing popularity of the automobile. Suddenly, however, the photographs become a type of narrative series; with the news of Ypres in April 1915, "the pictures alter – fill up with soldiers . . . . More and more people want to be seen. More and more people want to be remembered. Hundreds – thousands crowd into frame" (7). Findley is, of course, referring to the surge of young men offering to fight overseas after Ypres, eager for adventure, and fame – a continuing companion of the photograph. As he recently remarked: "everyone's fear" is "not to be one of those people chosen, *en passant*, to be hoarded in someone's memory; not to be a resident in someone else's country of invention" ("Countries" 106). The underlying irony in this natural human fear is the fact that these individual men are not hoarded in memory, but are, like Robert Ross, "obscured by violence."

From this public – almost sociological – reason for the departure of young men for the wars, Findley swiftly moves to an intensely private vision. Juxtaposed with these static photographs, in which all of the participants are "silenced at the edge of wharves and time" (7), is a "fiery image" of a private hell: *"Robert Ross comes riding straight towards the camera,"* his hands bleeding and his uniform on fire (7–8). This moving image seems to provide a living link between the researcher and the distant and mysterious world of the public photographs: *"He leaps through memory without a sound"* (8). Indeed, it is one of the "persistent images" of which Findley has spoken, for *"[y]ou know it will obtrude again and again until you find its meaning – here"* (8). Although John Hulcoop has suggested that the adverb "here" may "refer specifically to an *imaginary* photograph (since, so far as we know, no photographer is present to take pictures when Robert breaks out of the fired barn" ["Look! Listen!" 33]), I believe that the researcher is referring to the next object which he or she describes: the photograph which he or she has "here" in the archive. The "meaning" is to be found in this photograph because it reveals the meeting of a public and a private war – Robert Ross standing apart, watching a band play a military tune, "Soldiers of the Queen." The researcher interprets for us the private conflict lying beneath this seemingly innocent surface: "He's old enough to go to war. He hasn't gone. He doubts the validity in all this martialling of men but the doubt is inarticulate. It stammers in his brain" (8). At present, Robert is on the periphery; *The Wars* tells us why he suddenly clamours, like all of the anonymous men in the earlier photographs, "to crowd into frame" (7). Ironically, the reason is a private one – his feelings of guilt and grief about the death of his retarded sister, Rowena.

The photograph, therefore, is the major vehicle for explaining the motivations of those who went to the wars; it is, as well, a vehicle for revealing other subtle pressures which act upon Robert's mind. The photograph of the Ross's pony, entitled, *Meg – a Patriotic Pony*, because she is covered in bright bunting, reveals the vicious underside of patriotism. Meg is "either angry or frightened" (9), like the horses on the SS *Massanabie*, and in the background, Robert's younger brother Stuart, wearing Indian headdress, wields a baseball bat. When we later glimpse Stuart gleefully flying paper airplanes made out of Robert's letters from the front, we realize the horrifying complicity of those families at home who encouraged their young to be slaughtered in the name of patriotism or adventure. As Mrs. Ross asks, outside the church, "What does it mean – *to kill your children?* Kill them and then . . . go in there and sing about it!" (55).

In terms of character revelation, the photograph is an index both of superficiality and of sincerity. Lady Barbara D'Orsey is associated with the slick publicity photographs similar to those in *The Butterfly Plague.* "Her picture, like those of Cathleen Nesbitt and Lady Diana Manners, was 'everywhere' " (107). This public image – like the popularized image of the war – is clearly invidious. Eva-Marie Kröller, however, concludes that all "reproduction," whether of photographic images or of violence, "turns into a menace" (71). If one considers the private photographs in *The Wars*, however, one discovers that they are anything but menacing. The photograph of Barbara which Juliet D'Orsey owns reveals a truth not told in the publicity photographs. "You can see the sceptical eyes and the strange perpetual smile," confides Juliet. "It wasn't a smile at all. It was a nervous dimple on her left side" (112). Similarly, the "perpetual smile" which Barbara carries to a new lover once her old lover has been maimed in the war, may be less a sign of emotional poverty than a desperate, nervous flight from death to love. As Clive D'Orsey replies to Juliet, who asks why Robert and Barbara are so afraid: "everyone they've loved has died" (184). The private photograph reveals what the public photograph conceals, just as the private story of Robert Ross illuminates the tale of an entire generation.

Perhaps the most startling departure from Timothy Findley's earlier works in *The Wars* is his acceptance of some forms of fixity as positive and life-sustaining. Of course, the tortuous stasis of trench warfare is diametrically opposite; as the narrator baldly comments on the long-time British objectives in the Ypres region, "These were still objectives. Nothing had been won" (205). Fixity is the condition of the wounded men encased in body casts, such as Jamie Villiers, whom Barbara D'Orsey and Eugene Taffler visit. Fixity is also the emotional state within Barbara herself – a type of emotional stalemate. "And she was like that cold white vase and never said a word," recalls Juliet. "She stood and watched them dying like a stone. Ariadne and Dionysus" (116).

At the same time, however, permanence and fixity may carry positive emotional associations for Robert Ross and for Timothy Findley. " *'Robert?'* " asks Rowena, " *'Will you stay with me forever?'* " (18–19). This domestic permanence – the permanence of love – is denied Robert when Rowena dies in an accident. He is driven to the wars – to a negative type of fixity. On the railway platform, preparing to leave, Robert is "immobile .... resolutely still" (15). "How could he move?" the narrator asks. "Rowena had been buried the day before" (17). Part of Robert, then, dies with Rowena, but he nevertheless takes with him to the wars a permanent reminder of her: a photograph. Much later, after he has been raped by fellow officers – a symbol of Robert's ultimate betrayal by the war – he decides that this image of love and permanence can no longer exist in a world of hatred and death, and burns Rowena's photograph.

This conception of the photograph as the preserver of all that is precious and alive is clearly connected with the researcher's attempt to capture the essence of Robert Ross's life. In his or her documentary fervour, the researcher displays yet another positive form of fixity: the fixing of the past in order to celebrate it. The researcher's reverence for the photographic relics of that distant world is touching: "You turn them over – wondering if they'll spill [the people in the photograph] ... " (8). The researcher is, like us, not a first hand observer, unlike the people he or she interviews and fixes on tape, such as

Marian Turner and Juliet D'Orsey. He or she must therefore depend on photographs and tapes to recreate the memory of Robert Ross (unlike Marian Turner, who sends a photograph of herself to the researcher, explaining that "At my age, you don't need pictures any more" [224]). Photography therefore becomes a type of surrogate memory, and memories of life-sustaining acts of courage such as Robert Ross's desertion, Findley believes, are necessary in a violent world. "Memory," he recently wrote, "provides a ground ... on which we can face reality, accommodate reality and, possibly, even survive it" ("Countries" 106). Memory, therefore, is the ultimate answer to the question, "How does one face a terrifying reality?", which Findley poses in works such as *The Butterfly Plague*.

This increased importance of memory in Findley's mind largely accounts for his reevaluation of man's relationship to the photograph in *The Wars*. One notes that the associations between guns and photographs in *The Last of the Crazy People* are absent in *The Wars*. Next to Robert's photograph in the Ross house lies a wooden box containing not a gun but letters – apt symbols of Findley's belief in the power of document and memory to preserve the spirit of the dead. *"Dead men are serious – that's what this photograph is striving to say .... I lived – was young – and died"* (49).

The final proof of Findley's belief in the association of memory and photography occurs in the epilogue of the novel, where we are presented with two photographs of Robert: Robert with an animal skull, and Robert with Rowena. These two photographs represent Robert's all-encompassing love – his love for the creatures of the earth, and his love for fellow human beings. Beyond this generalization, however, each of these photographs yields a further truth. The image of Robert holding an animal skull has been interpreted as a symbol of fate; for Peter Klovan the skull "may well symbolize his [Robert's] destiny, for it is one of several images of the frail and the delicate" (62–63), and for Michael Taylor it represents Robert's "bleak future" (174). I would argue, however, that the photograph suggests memory and preservation rather than grim fate, on the basis that the image of a man or woman holding a skull, in traditional pictorial iconography, is an example of *memento mori* – a powerful reminder of death. Moreover, in terms of the iconography of this photograph, we note that Robert holds the skull in his right hand, while on his left there stands a forbidding "fascio of guns" (226). The gun and the animal suggest the elements which meet and do battle in war – the life-destroying and the living. The skull is, of course, a stark reminder of which element is likelier to gain the upper hand in the conflict between the two. Yet the skull is also an archaeological relic – like the photograph – a reminder that "I lived – was young – and died." This bizarre truth, that the fact of death brings home to us the value of life, is captured in the words of the essayist which the researcher then recalls: *"the spaces between the perceiver and the thing perceived can . . . be closed with a shout of recognition. One form of a shout is a shot. Nothing so completely verifies our perception of a thing as our killing of it"* (226).

In *The Wars*, Findley offers us a positive and creative alternative to the "shot" that destroys life (which we have already witnessed at the end of *The Last of the Crazy People*) – that is, the photographic "shot" which preserves it. In the very last photograph of *The Wars*, showing Robert holding Rowena on a pony, we witness one such life-preserving shot. "On the back is written: 'Look! you can see our breath!' And," the narrator affirms, "you can" (226). Eva-Marie Kröller believes that this final statement "matches in ambiguity that of another highly regarded Canadian novel, Sinclair Ross's *As for Me and My House* " (68) in which Mrs. Bentley ends her diary with the statement: "That's right, Philip. I want it so." Kröller's interpretation is, of course, based on her negative view of photography in *The Wars*; for her, the comfort offered by this photograph is undercut by the knowledge of Robert's death, and by the storyteller's final incapacity to recreate for us a complete picture of Robert Ross. Nevertheless, to put this issue in perspective, one must examine the remainder of Findley's already-mentioned comments to Johan Aitken about the photograph's relation to life: "I still sit with a photograph and I think, if I could only get in there with you, I could walk in there, and that person is saying something, that moment in there, and one never, never, never dies." Indeed, the photograph becomes a type of Keatsian Grecian urn for Findley, for it can "bring life back that's gone, and dissect and keep the dead alive, amongst us, which is very important" (Aitken 83). Therefore, the last photograph in *The Wars* affirms that human life, like the frozen breath of Robert and Rowena, may be captured by the processes of memory and writing, and shown to be, paradoxically, both ephemeral and everlasting.

✦ *Famous Last Words* (1981) ✦

The conflict between the ephemeral and the everlasting – the frail and vulnerable human life and the enduring spirit of man – once again captures Findley's imagination in *Famous Last Words*. As we read the writing of Hugh Selwyn Mauberley on the walls of the Austrian hotel along with Lieutenant Quinn, we are constantly aware that the mangled body of the man who experienced all of these sensations lies a few yards away, "obscured by violence" like Robert Ross, and yet curiously alive in the fictional document of his life. As in *The Wars*, photography – not exclusively film, as Eugene Benson argues (602) – reveals this meeting of the momentary and the eternal, of fiction and history.

As in *The Butterfly Plague*, photography is associated with a destructive type of fiction – lies. Mauberley is repeatedly described as the subject of countless newspaper photographs – photographs which reveal him to be on apparently intimate terms with the rich and powerful, in particular Wallis Simpson. One of his personal friends, Diana Allenby (daughter of an actual historical figure, Field Marshall Allenby), is identified by "her famous smile that is seen in all the Beaton photographs" (90). Publicity photographs such as these are unmasked by Mauberley himself. Speaking of the photographs taken of the King's and Wallis's circle before the abdication, Mauberley wryly reflects: "Everyone in all those pictures taken then was smiling; everyone was radiant; everyone was infallible. It was all a lie, of course." The photograph is here a manipulative device; by making it appear as though "the *people*" approved of Edward's and Wallis's attachment, the King could then pressure the rest of the royal family to approve of his marriage. Mauberley realizes that he has taken part in an historical masquerade; he has been one of those smiling figures who believed that "ours was the ultimate face of the age" (98). Fiction, in this case, proves more dependable than the photographic document; Ezra Pound, in his poem "Hugh Selwyn

Mauberley," maintains that the true symbol of the age was not a glossy smile but an "accelerated grimace" (188).

One photograph in particular demonstrates this uneasy tension between history and fiction. Immediately before meeting with Wallis Simpson to encourage her to join the international Nazi cabal, Mauberley reveals that a famous photograph of Edward VIII riding in a Daimler at Nice is, in fact, a photograph of himself hiding behind a newspaper blow-up of Edward's smiling face (143). The face of Mauberley is, indeed, absent from the pages of history, for he is a fictional character. This sense of fictionality is further underlined by the fact that Mauberley's photograph of Edward appears in the only major newspaper which does not print photographs – *Le Monde*. Yet perhaps this photograph is Findley's way of suggesting that under the regal façade of the head of state may lurk a fascist sympathizer. Findley may also be suggesting through this collage of historical and fictional "faces" that the figure of Mauberley – and fiction – may disclose a human truth which is not always available to us through historical documentation.

On one occasion, Findley quotes with enthusiasm Marie-Claire Blais's description of the writer as *un témoin* – a witness ("The Countries of Invention" 106). In *Famous Last Words*, as in *The Last of the Crazy People*, Findley grants his protagonist a camera-like perception, but unlike Hooker Winslow, Mauberley also has an ability to sort and interpret those perceptions. Mauberley is a self-avowed "compulsive witness" who cannot "refrain from setting things down on paper, recording the lives of those around him, moment by moment – every word and every gesture instantly frozen in his private cipher" (21). This all-inclusive vision can lead to artistic amoralism, and yet Mauberley, unlike the publicity photographers, seems to sense that "in this microcosmic hell the age I lived in was being defined, and if I wanted to write then I had to force myself to become a witness to these lives and these events and to this place" (68). Nevertheless, Mauberley, like Pound, in spite of his vision of a contemporary hell, becomes enmeshed in the fascist cause. His flight, and his decision to write his testament on the walls of the hotel, place him, as a writer, closer to his former enemy, the documentary writer Julia Franklin, who in camera-like fashion "never knowingly lied. Which is why ... she could be extremely dangerous" (122).

Mauberley becomes every bit as dangerous a witness to his times; in a final grim twist of irony his Nazi assassin drives an ice pick through his eye.

Mauberley's act of writing is both dangerous and crucial because it could change forever the accepted truths of history. Writers, Findley has claimed, "witness and record ... the cryptic passage of people and events that, otherwise, would gain no place in memory" ("Countries" 106). Visual images in *Famous Last Words*, as in *The Wars*, are important analogues to these processes of writing and remembering. Visiting the caves at Altamira, Mauberley is suddenly struck by the curious persistence into the present of the lives of men and women long dead: "And out of the corner of my eye I caught a glimpse of something irresistible above my head ... the imprint of a human hand .... And I knew I was sitting at the heart of the human race – which is its will to say *I am*" (172-73). Mauberley, like the researcher in *The Wars*, encounters here a delicate reminder of man's endurance – a visual ancestor of the photograph of Robert and Rowena on a horse – and he fittingly reproduces it alongside his own art work, on the walls of the hotel.

Here, as in *The Wars*, Findley is aware that the belief in the value of human life is often sparked by our consciousness of man's cruelty to man. Therefore, Captain Freyberg's horrifying photographs of Dachau are a necessary part of Quinn's reconstruction of the story – and of ours:

> "I know you were there," said Freyberg. "But do you remember?"
> "Yes; I remember. God damn it, sir. And I don't want to see those bloody things again. I can see them in my mind. I don't need any bloody photographs."
> "Everyone needs photographs, Quinn." (390)

Critics of Findley have tended to side overwhelmingly with Lieutenant Quinn in this debate, seeing Captain Freyberg as, in John Hulcoop's terms, a Gradgrind figure who only wants "facts, facts, facts" ("The Will to Be" 119). It is true that Freyberg is obsessed – almost driven crazy – by the thought of Dachau, to the extent that he cannot bear to read Mauberley's account with any objectivity. Yet Findley is surely suggesting

here that viewing history as a fiction has dangerous consequences as well. Throughout *Famous Last Words*, Quinn has read
Mauberley's account with sympathy and intelligence and yet he
has, until this point, refused to look at the mangled body of
Mauberley. Similarly, one of Freyberg's photographs is "a
picture of Quinn himself .... standing beside an open oven
door – and inside the oven twenty bodies, or thirty, unburned"
(390), a description which recreates an actual photograph from
Dachau (see fig. 4). Quinn – like all human beings – cannot
remain an impassive observer; his literal response to the
photograph: "Can't you see I'm standing right there," shows
that he has not properly understood the crucial word "remember," as Freyberg – and Findley – use it. "Yes," Freyberg
reiterates. "But do you remember it?" (390). Memory, then,
involves active participation and self-examination; after this
confrontation with Freyberg, Quinn looks for the first time at
Mauberley's body, and reaches out to touch and "take" his own
memento mori – Mauberley's scarf, which he entwines around
his neck. Fiction, therefore, is never entirely free of history; as
Freyberg insists (unlike Marian Turner of *The Wars*), we need
photographs just as we need to remember.

✦ Recent Short Fiction & *Not Wanted on the Voyage* (1984) ✦

Findley's recent works attest to the fact that we need – ever
more desperately in an age where destruction seems imminent
– to remember. Nevertheless, there still appear those characters
in Findley's fiction who cannot confront the passage of time. In
"Dinner Along the Amazon," Conrad changes his appearance
entirely by applying egg white to his face, creating a homemade
face-lift (an image reminiscent of the cosmetic and psychological masks of the Duchess in *Famous Last Words*). He jokingly
enters a dinner party to the accompaniment of a song called
"Traces": *"A faded photograph, / Covered, now, with lines and
creases ... "* (*Dinner* 246). Conrad's other attempts to escape the
past are similarly futile; Olivia sees her husband's friend as
"[p]oor deadly Conrad, dragging the unwelcome past with all
its frayed address books and stringy love affairs behind him
... " (232). As the image of the photograph suggests, the past is
not so easily discarded.

In *Not Wanted on the Voyage*, Findley takes his concern with history, fiction, and seeing to a startling conclusion: he retells the story of Noah, rendering the patriarch a type of fascist ruler who, although he knows that Jehova has died in sorrow because of the world's decadence, builds his ark nevertheless – and a hierarchical ark at that, with certain family members and living creatures relegated to the lower, darker regions of the hold, like the horses on the SS *Massanabie* in *The Wars*. The tale is, as Findley gleefully admits, full of anachronisms (Fitzgerald), but photography is not one of them. Nevertheless, many of the motifs which we have seen associated with photography are interwoven once again in this novel. Vision, for instance, is all-important, as the epigraph, from Phyllis Webb's poem "Leaning," clearly demonstrates:

> And you, are you still here
> tilting in this stranded ark
>   blind and seeing in the dark.

Findley transforms this image of the blind prophet into the figure of Mrs. Noyes's cat, Mottyl, who, although feeble and increasingly blind, is perceptive enough to abhor the inhumanity and dogmatism of Noah. Indeed, Noah's scientific experiments have been responsible for Mottyl's blindness – one of many signs in the novel that Findley is speaking not only about the ancient deluge, but about the technological deluge to come.

In this conflict between technological vision and the enduring vision of living creatures, memory once again plays a decisive part. Lucy, Findley's mischievous recreation of Lucifer as an ally of the oppressed creatures, is its major spokesperson. After the brutal killing of the unicorn, symbolizing the destruction of the imagination by a narrow rationalism, Lucy argues that "All the moments of this creature's life can be with us in an instant. All we have to do is remember it alive. If we can forget its death – it will live" (280). As in *Famous Last Words*, however, death cannot be ignored; after a brief moment of resuscitation, the unicorn once again dies. Findley's narrator relates this phoenix-like rebirth to mankind's fluctuating capacity to believe in the imagination: "Just as people either did or didn't – could or couldn't – would or wouldn't return to the memory of the moment when the Unicorn was flesh and blood and lived in the wood at the bottom of Noah's Hill" (281). As in the scene at the Altamira caves in *Famous Last Words*, memory becomes the preserver of human existence and imagination; it brings to life all of the unicorns which have been banished from our world.

The gradual transformation of the photograph in Findley's writing, from a symbol of stasis and death to that of the guardian of the human imagination under siege, clearly parallels Findley's own growing insistence on the primacy of memory. In a sense, Timothy Findley undergoes a development similar to that of his heroine Cassandra Wakelin in *Can You See Me Yet?*, who, upon being confronted with the fact that her photographs are false, persists in treasuring them nevertheless because they are, for her, true fictions. Timothy Findley's photographs, in the words of his fictional character Hugh Selwyn Mauberley, allow us to see into "the heart of the human race – which is its will to say *I am*" (172–73).

Chapter Three

✛

" The Making and Destroying ": The Photographic Image in Michael Ondaatje's Works

"Nothing so completely verifies our perception of a thing as our killing of it" (*Wars* 226). The words of Timothy Findley's imaginary essayist, Nicholas Fagan, in the closing pages of *The Wars*, could easily serve as an epigraph to the works of another Canadian postmodernist writer, Michael Ondaatje. Ondaatje's fascination with the hazy borderline between analytical perception and destruction is manifest in both his poetry and his fiction. In *The Collected Works of Billy the Kid* (1970) and *Coming Through Slaughter* (1976), Ondaatje voices the conviction that the camera is an agent of fixity even more emphatically than Findley does in his work. Nevertheless, Ondaatje, like Findley, can never quite escape the other side of the photographic paradox: that photography bears positive associations with human memory and that the photographer's art is therefore analogous to that of the writer. Ondaatje's *Running in the Family* (1982) occupies a position in the development of his view of photography roughly analogous to that of Findley's *The Wars*; it marks his full awareness of photography as both destroyer and preserver.

The remarkable similarities between Ondaatje's development as a writer and that of Timothy Findley are partly due to their similar interest in visual art. Ondaatje is a photographer and a film-maker, yet he also displays a lively interest in twentieth-century painting in his poetry and criticism. He commented to Sam Solecki, for instance, that his long poem, *The*

Man with Seven Toes (1969), was inspired by a series of paintings by Sidney Nolan on a story of an Englishwoman rescued from cannibals by a convict – the same story which inspired Patrick White's *A Fringe of Leaves* (1976). The resulting poem is serial in nature, like the Nolan paintings, and is described by Ondaatje as "brief and imagistic" ("Interview" 47). Ondaatje's favourite painter, however, if one is to judge from his poetry, is Henri Rousseau: "Having to put forward candidates for God / I nominate Henri Rousseau and Dr. Bucke" (*Rat Jelly* 66). Ondaatje's pairing of the French naïve painter with the author of *Cosmic Consciousness* (1901), indicates that he is fascinated by the mystic aspect of Rousseau's work. In many of Rousseau's canvases, *The Dream*, for instance, this mysticism is partly derived from the eerily static nature of the scene – a mixture also found in many of Ondaatje's poems.

Ondaatje's sense of affinity with certain painters is borne out by the terminology which his critics frequently employ when describing his poetry. *The Collected Works of Billy the Kid* has been christened a "montage" (Blott 188), a "collage" (Scobie, "*Coming Through Slaughter*" 5), and an experiment in "mixed media" (Moss, *A Reader's Guide* 224). Each of these terms is derived from criticism of modern or contemporary art from the time of Bracque and Picasso to the present. Moreover, Ondaatje, like Alice Munro, has been called a magic realist or magic naturalist, most recently by Leslie Mundwiler, who argues: "the imagery [of Ondaatje's poems] is generally a vivid depiction of, or extrapolation from, natural detail ... " (130). Mundwiler's subsequent argument, that one needs "oxymoronic terms such as 'magical naturalism' and 'naturalistic fatalism' " because Ondaatje's use of imagery "does not rest on a coherent philosophical vision" (131), is less defensible. To choose one example among many, Billy the Kid's seemingly surrealistic thoughts while dying actually rest on a firm and demonstrable thematic basis:

> ... lovely perfect sun balls
> breaking at each other click
> click click click like Saturday morning pistol cleaning
> (*Collected Works* 95)

Billy's last perceptions ironically link suns and guns, a grim reminder of the growing mechanization and loss of humanity which have plagued Billy throughout his life. This vision – described by Dennis Lee as "the strife of world and earth," a "structural model of planet" which he terms "savage fields" (11) – constitutes Ondaatje's coherent philosophical vision.

Even in his work as a critic, Michael Ondaatje frequently uses analogies to painting to clarify the underlying philosophy of a writer's work. Of Leonard Cohen he writes: *"Let Us Compare Mythologies* is, then, a book of moods: a world of 'Lunch on the Grass,' 'Olympia' or Tissot" (*Leonard Cohen* 14).

For Ondaatje, writing and the visual arts collaborate in yet another distinct artistic activity: book design. As the careful orchestration of spaces and lines on the pages of *The Collected Works of Billy the Kid* attest, visual effect is as important to Ondaatje the poet as it was to e.e. cummings. "The presentation of the poem is very important to me," he explained to Sam Solecki, "the printing itself is an art form." In fact, he sees the making of a book and the making of a film as similar projects: "I find the editing of a manuscript to be like the editing of a film, that's when you determine the work's shape, rhythmic structure ..." ("Interview" 47–48). Ondaatje therefore takes an active part in the selection of type, paper, and the placing of photographs; his own aesthetic dislike for poems which carry over onto the next page thus influences the overall visual nature of his works (and may account, in part, for his preference for "brief," "imagistic" lyrics). Ironically, such formal innovation draws puzzled responses from more print-oriented readers; one critic of *The Man with Seven Toes*, although realizing that the placing of stark lyrics on a wide, short page might bear some thematic significance, complained that the book would cause no end of trouble to bibliophiles attempting to place it on their shelves because of its unusual size.

Ondaatje's sensitivity to space and composition is doubtless a result of his work in film and theatre. "I was brought up on movies and song!" he writes in his most recent collection, published in 1984, *Secular Love*, "Educated at the Bijou" (40–41). Although Ondaatje has not written screenplays for any of his works (unlike Timothy Findley, who wrote the screenplay for Robin Phillips's version of *The Wars*), he has adapted two of his works, *The Collected Works of Billy the Kid* and *Coming Through*

Slaughter, for the stage. Ondaatje is better known, however, for his original films, *Sons of Captain Poetry* (1970) and *The Clinton Special* (1974). Ondaatje's comments about the latter, a film of Theatre Passe Muraille's *The Farm Show* which was performed before an audience in Clinton, Ontario, reveal a concern with artistic control which pervades all of his work:

> Talking about the director of a documentary film strikes me as invalid cos [sic] ... everything is left up to the camera-man, the lighting man, the actors and the people you are actually interviewing. I think it's very dangerous to try to over-control that; when you try and control it into a certain point of view then you get the CBC kind of documentary which knows what it's going to say before the actual filming begins. (Solecki, "Interview" 41)

One instantly thinks of Timothy Findley's acerbic exposé of over-controlled documentary art in *The Paper People* (itself, ironically, a CBC production). Ondaatje does not suggest, however, that the film-maker should dispose entirely of all traditional notions of form and composition; rather, he points out: "With the actual editing that's when the director moves in. That's when you decide the film's structure" (Solecki, "Interview" 41). Interestingly, the same interplay between control and freedom is evident in Ondaatje's poetry and fiction. His lyrics, although they appear to be free from rhythmic patterning, for example, still depend on rhythmic inversions and other techniques for much of their power:

> I, a moving silk,
> bubbles draining from my skull
> would twist down
> with black ugly feet
> and my hair would toss
> slow, like grass.
>
> (*The Dainty Monsters* 51)

The spondee in the third line emphasizes the downward movement, and the stress on "slow" literally forces the reader to slow down while reading. Thus, it could be said of Ondaatje, as Frank Lewis says of Buddy Bolden in *Coming Through Slaughter*: "We thought he was formless, but I think now he was tormented by order . . . " (37).

Ondaatje's other major film, *Sons of Captain Poetry*, explicitly comments on this symbiotic relationship between film and writing. It is significant that Ondaatje chooses a visual form to talk about a primarily visual poet; bpNichol. As he explained to Sam Solecki: "I had wanted to write something on nichol and I'd realized that you couldn't really *write* about concrete poetry, that it had to be expressed in another form." In addition, *Sons of Captain Poetry* represented to Ondaatje a flight away from the exclusivity of language. "I'd just finished the actual writing of *The Collected Works of Billy the Kid*," Ondaatje recalls, "and there was a real sense of words meaning nothing to me anymore, and I was going around interpreting things into words . . . . It was a very dangerous thing for me mentally . . . . I just felt I had to go into another field, something totally visual" ("Interview" 40). The same fear of the hegemony of the word is evident in other postmodernist writers; one thinks, for example, of John Barth's attack (ironically a verbal one) on his readers in *Lost in the Funhouse*: "You . . . print-oriented bastard . . . " (123). Leslie Mundwiler, too, observes that *Sons of Captain Poetry* is not only about bpNichol, but about Michael Ondaatje as well. In terms which recall Findley's *The Paper People*, he calls the film a combination of "the critic's attempt to make sense of a poetic enterprise with the poet's own selection, utterance and performance for the quiet eye of the camera" (116) – a meeting of the verbal and the visual, of the silent and the aural.

Ondaatje's use of a passage written by Peter Handke as an epigraph to *Secular Love* is an imaginative application of the language of film to the writing of poetry: "You always hold back something of yourself," the young actor is told, "even when you yawn you're afraid to open your mouth all the way . . . . I'm looking forward to seeing you grow older from film to film" (7). The words could apply equally to Ondaatje's development as a writer, to his gradual willingness to approach his personal past through his poems and fiction. Critics of those poems and fictional works have not been slow to note their resemblance to the medium of film. Gary Geddes and Phyllis Bruce flatly state that "Ondaatje's poems have a number of things in common with films": they are visual, dramatic, concerned with detail and "angles of vision," and they tend to deal with "extreme, or, at least, uncommon" people or places (289). Sam Solecki notes that Ondaatje's books "don't so much end as dissolve suggestively back into the author" in a way reminiscent of a final fadeout in film ("Michael Ondaatje" 82). *The Collected Works of Billy the Kid*, in particular, has sparked a great deal of interdisciplinary comparison; T.D. MacLulich observes that "[m]uch of *The Collected Works* consists of Billy re-playing scenes from his past" or visualizing "scenes from an unusual viewpoint, rather like a film director experimenting with camera angles ..." (113). Perry Nodelman provides a concrete example of this film-like quality; lines 1 to 6 of a poem describing Billy's removal of a bullet from a man's stomach are repeated in reverse order, "like a film run backwards," show-ing, according to Nodelman, Billy's attempt to replay past experiences and thus purge himself of them (70). Even the subtitle of the collection, *Left Handed Poems*, is, according to Stephen Scobie, a reference to film – to Arthur Penn's film about Billy the Kid entitled *The Left-Handed Gun* ("Two Authors" 225). Such observations lend credence to Ondaatje's own claim that "with *Billy the Kid* I was trying to make the film I couldn't afford to shoot, in the form of a book" (Solecki, "Interview" 46).

Ondaatje's use of film to comment on a fellow poet's work does not end with *Sons of Captain Poetry*; his book on Leonard Cohen contains several references to film. There, Ondaatje applies his own belief in the relationship between manuscript-editing and film-making, to Cohen's poetry. "The very strict editing in the writing," argues Ondaatje of *The Favourite Game*, "is also partly a result of the influence of films" ... (27). Breavman's story is "dramatic" (26), resembling "a film-script"; chapters "fade out" (13) in much the same way that Solecki claims the endings of Ondaatje's books do. In addition Ondaatje cannot resist making direct comparisons between elements of Cohen's works and his own particular film favourites. The women in *Let Us Compare Mythologies*, for example, remind Ondaatje of a scene in Richard Lester's *The Knack* (13), and the early poems' mixture of tragedy and farce recall to Ondaatje's mind the movie *Shoot the Piano Player* (23). Film, therefore, enters into every aspect of Michael Ondaatje's creative life, even more emphatically and obsessively than for Timothy Findley, who has stronger ties than Ondaatje to other performance arts such as theatre and dance. Nevertheless, the concern of both artists with the relationship between moving image and word, and with the role of the artist as researcher, suggests that they reflect a worldwide trend in recent fiction noted by Robert Alter:

> Film, because it is a collaborative artistic enterprise involving a complicated chain of technical procedures, almost invites attention to its constitutive processes .... The close parallels between what is happening now in the two media suggest that the self-consciousness of both may reflect a heightened new stage of modern culture's general commitment to knowing all that can be known about its own components and dynamics. (219–20)

Closely allied to this postmodernist fascination with cine-matic technique and words is Ondaatje's lively interest in still photography. A photographer of some talent himself, Ondaatje has tried to bring the sense of stasis created by still photography into the moving, sequential medium of film. Of *The Clinton Special*, Ondaatje commented: "I wanted that sense throughout the film that each shot would almost be a static photograph." Ondaatje accomplished this by using sepia-coloured tones in certain shots. The final result of this merging of visual tech-niques Ondaatje christened "talking photography" (Solecki, "Interview" 42) – a striking parallel to Timothy Findley's statement: "yes everybody, photographs can be heard ..." (Aitken 80). In *Sons of Captain Poetry*, Ondaatje uses actual photographs in a scene in which Nichol comments in a voice-over on his family. In making *The Clinton Special*, howev-er, Ondaatje chose for one scene dealing with the rural character Charlie Wilson *not* to show an actual photograph of Charlie. "We were looking for photographs of him when we were shooting," recalls Ondaatje, "but I'm glad ... that we didn't find any cos [sic] he becomes more detailed just cos he is so abstract ... it's left up to the imagination and it's preferable that way" (Solecki, "Interview" 44). This dual response to the photograph – as a key to memory, kinship, and personal history, and as a severe restraint on human imagination – resurfaces in Ondaatje's later fiction.

"I'm very interested in photography," Ondaatje admitted to Sam Solecki ("Interview" 42), and this interest almost overshadows his interest in film and painting reflected in his critical work. In his study of Leonard Cohen, references to photography outnumber those to painting and film. "It is not just the reliance on film that gives *The Favourite Game* a visual rather than a literary style," he explains at one point. "Cohen constantly uses photographs . . . . " Ondaatje places particular emphasis on the ways in which Cohen's style may be said to be photographic. Of *The Favourite Game*, again, he writes: "We are not guided along a cohesive time sequence but are shown segments from scrapbooks, home movies, diaries – all of which flash in front of us like 'those uncertain images that were always flashing in his mind' " (24). Note the similarity between Ondaatje's description and Timothy Findley's vision of *The Wars* as a long road with billboards along the way, flashing the photographs which represent the significant moments of Robert Ross's life. Ondaatje even uses photographic metaphors when speaking of Cohen's work, seeing *Parasites of Heaven* as "a series of mental photographs" (59) and *The Favourite Game* as "a beautiful book" to which one returns "several times as one returns to a photograph album" (34). The work is, in his eyes, "an autobiography of Breavman told in the third person, like one of those group photographs with a white circle drawn around the central character" (28). This obsessive image of the group photograph resurfaces in both of his major works of fiction – *Coming Through Slaughter* and *Running in the Family*.

"*I send you a picture* . . . . " The opening words of *The Collected Works of Billy the Kid* (5) speak compellingly of Michael Ondaatje's aims and methods. In order to place the photographs in *Coming Through Slaughter* and *Running in the Family* in context, one must first examine the associations which Ondaatje makes with photography in his poetry.

Reading through Ondaatje's poems, from *The Dainty Monsters* (1967) to *Secular Love* (1984), one cannot ignore his obsession with the conflict between artistic fixity and the flux of experience – a conflict which he, like Timothy Findley and Alice Munro, associates with photography. In Ondaatje, however, this conflict becomes the overriding concern of the work. In "Four Eyes," from *The Dainty Monsters*, the speaker glimpses a photograph and a painting through the eyes of his lover, and is driven to record "this moment" – to compete with the power of the camera and the brush to capture a slice of time:

> I would freeze this moment
> and in supreme patience
> place pianos
> and craggy black horses on a beach
> and in immobilised time
> attempt to reconstruct. (46)

Even in these early lyrics, the desire for artistic fixity becomes an obsessive theme; in "The Time Around Scars," the speaker reflects: "We remember the time around scars, / They freeze irrelevant emotions" (*Dainty Monsters* 49), much in the manner of a photograph.

In later collections, such as *Rat Jelly* (1973), this fascination continues. "King Kong Meets Wallace Stevens" is an allegory of the meeting of flux and fixity. The reader is invited to "[t]ake two photographs": one a static image of the "portly, benign" poet, and the other a moving photograph of Kong "staggering / lost in New York streets again." The photographs represent two impulses – artistic creation and animalistic destruction – which the poet senses within himself ("Is it significant that I eat bananas as I write this?"). The photograph of Stevens, however, suggests the possibility of poetry allowing one to exorcise this destructive impulse, allowing one to fix experience and yet retain its fluidity: "Meanwhile W. S. in his suit / is thinking chaos is thinking fences" (61). Ondaatje later addresses this conflict between chaos and fences in greater depth in *Coming Through Slaughter*.

In "Burning Hills," from the same collection, a group photograph (the earliest example of this recurrent motif in Ondaatje's work) "fuses the 5 summers" of the writer's adolescence in one static image:

> Eight of them are leaning against a wall
> . . . .
> looking into the camera and the sun

trying to smile at the unseen adult photographer
. . . .
Except one who was eating an apple. That was him
oblivious to the significance of the moment.
Now he hungers to have that arm around the next
    shoulder.
The wretched apple is fresh and white. (58)

The indirect glance of the young writer suggests both unaware-
ness of the moment, and evasion, in contrast to the direct gazes
of his companions. The grown writer's longing for the fixed
moment of the past – the partially eaten apple of experience – is
powerfully captured in the epithet "wretched." In *Rat Jelly*,
poetry becomes the agent which is able to fix without rendering
the subject lifeless or bland (the agent, if you will, which makes
jelly of the rat, but does not allow us to forget that "it's rat /
steamy dirty hair and still alive" [31]). Voiced in another (less
gruesome) way, this type of poetic capturing resembles

   . . . a blurred photograph of a gull.
   Caught vision. The stunning white bird
   an unclear stir.

   And that is all this writing should be then.
   The beautiful formed things caught at the wrong
       moment
   so they are shapeless, awkward
   moving to the clear
                    ("The Gate in His Head," *Rat Jelly* 62)

In the later poems in *There's a Trick with a Knife I'm Learning
to Do* (1979), Ondaatje turns his attention to another element of
the past which he must also "fix": his Sri Lankan childhood.
Writing of "Uswetakeiyawa," a place where the imagination
and the subconscious seem ready to surface at any moment, he
describes "A landscape nightmare / unphotographed country"
(90). *Running in the Family* will be his attempt to capture in
words and photographs this untouched land of his past.

The past is, in fact, the other main element which Ondaatje
associates with photography in his poetry. In "Tink, Summer
Rider," the photograph of a girl on a horse, "her hair turned by

102

wind," contrasts sharply with the image of the "serious," "rigid" woman that girl later becomes (*Dainty Monsters* 40). The photograph thus becomes a poignant reminder of the lost wildness of youth – and, by extension, the lost wildness of human beings as a result of civilizing forces. This association is borne out in "Burning Hills" from *Rat Jelly*, where the lost summers of the writer's youth are also "layers of civilization in his memory / ... old photographs he didn't look at anymore" (57).

In his recent poems Ondaatje more often associates the personal past, rather than the past of the species, with photographs. "Light," probably the best of the newer poems in *There's a Trick with a Knife I'm Learning to Do*, is a poetic ancestor of Ondaatje's *Running in the Family*. The poet replays in his mind, as though in a darkened room: "Those relatives in my favourite slides / re-shot from old minute photographs so they now stand / complex ambiguous grainy on my wall" (105). As in "Uswetakeiyawa," the poet desires to "fix" or come to terms with these ambiguous or troubling images from the past: "These are their fragments, all I remember, / wanting more knowledge of them ... " (107). Photographs of the past and present merge in the poet's mind; a beloved photograph of his mother and uncle in fancy dress calls to mind "A picture of my kids at Halloween" which "has the same contact and laughter" (106). Here is the merging of fixity and flux which Ondaatje has spoken of in earlier poems; the fixed and faded people in these photographs come alive because they are part of a human chain: "In the mirror and in my kids / I see them in my flesh" (107). These ancestors are, in fact, the opposite of the shadowy, removed photographic ancestors at whom Timothy Findley's Hooker Winslow gazes in *The Last of the Crazy People*. Ondaatje's concept of a living continuity unfreezes these portraits and gives them life.

The Collected Works of Billy the Kid (1970) is on the borderline between Ondaatje's poetry and fiction, for it contains both poems and prose. Moreover, it marks Ondaatje's first sustained use of photography as a structural device. The collection is, in essence, a series of visual and verbal photographs; it has been likened to "a series of lenses, all wide open to admit a multiplicity of impressions" of Billy (Blott 201). The overall effect of reading the collection is similar to that of looking through a prism; our vision of Billy shifts, new highlights are visible according to our position as a viewer – standing either alongside Sallie Chisum or Sherriff Garrett.

Throughout the collection, Ondaatje uses photography as a metaphor for this crucial choice of perspective. The opening section, based on an actual diary entry of the frontier photographer L.A. Huffman, creates an immediate impression of scientific accuracy: *"I send you a picture of Billy made with the Perry shutter as quick as it can be worked,"* he boasts, and is quick to add that his photographs of horses *"were made with the lens wide open and many of the best exposed when my horse was in motion"* (5). Here we meet once again the conflicting elements of fixity and flux in Ondaatje's poetry. The experiments with photographing a horse in motion are based on experiments carried out by American photographers Eadweard Muybridge and Thomas Eakins (a photograph of a man on a horse by the former appropriately appears on the cover of Ondaatje's collection). Critics such as Stephen Scobie and Perry Nodelman have noted the appropriateness of an image of multiple exposure and analysis to the structure of the collection. What must also be pointed out is the fact that both Muybridge and Ondaatje are seeking to alter a legend or lie – in Muybridge's case it is the belief that a horse extends all four legs off the ground at once when galloping. Similarly, Ondaatje is contravening all of the glamorous versions of the Billy the Kid legend (one of which he includes for purposes of ironic contrast, "Billy the Kid and the Princess") in order to study Billy as the prototype of a certain type of artist – a potential creator who becomes a destroyer.

The element within Billy which makes him a destroyer rather than a creative artist is his suffocating sense of fixity – a condition which Ondaatje persistently explores through the use of the photographic image. Billy is consistently linked with images of mechanization as opposed to organic life – what Dennis Lee would term the images of "world" as opposed to "earth." We have already witnessed the two main images of mechanization in Timothy Findley's *The Last of the Crazy People*: the camera and the gun. "I am very still," Billy thinks at one point, "I take in all the angles of the room" (21). Not only is Billy a silent human camera, but a human gun as well. "He never uses his left hand for anything except of course to shoot," recalls Patrick Garrett. "He said he did fingers exercises subconsciously. . . . From then on I noticed his left hand churning within itself, each finger circling alternately like a train wheel" (43). In addition, Billy's words, "I caught Charlie Bowdre dying," have been interpreted as yet another example of Billy's desire to make things stand still (Nodelman 73). One thinks also of a chilling remark made by the famous war photographer, Robert Capa, that he "got" the picture of the last Allied soldier to die in the Second World War.

Throughout the collection, this mechanical fixity is continually undermined by the flux and chaos of experience. During the night spent drinking with the Chisums and Garrett, Billy recalls a picture taken of him, with "a white block down the fountain road where somebody had come out of a building . . . and ridden away . . . " Billy, on the other hand, is immobile, enslaved to a machine, "waiting standing still for the acid in the camera to dry firm" (68). A photograph taken by Daguerre forty years earlier provides a striking analogue to this scene; it shows an apparently deserted street in Paris, with only one human figure in sight – a man having his shoes polished. Since in 1839, when this picture was taken, "the length of time required to obtain a daguerreotype image ranged from five to sixty minutes," all of the other people walking along the street were moving too quickly to have their image fixed on the plate (Rosenblum 17). The tiny figure of the man, like Billy, is a haunting image of fixity amid a world of flux.

One of the few occasions when we see Billy breaking out of this mechanical stasis is in a moment of inebriation – a moment when the subconscious is likely to escape its vigilant censors. Chewing red-dirt marijuana, Billy once again thinks of a photograph, "the only one I had then." This portrait of Billy pumping water – which freezes a continuous motion – becomes, for an instant, a moving picture: "Only now, with the red dirt, water started dripping out of the photo" (50).

There is a wide range of responses among critics of *The Collected Works*, to this conflict between fixity and flux, and the role which photography plays in that conflict. T.D. MacLulich asks: "should the book be construed as a warning against the dehumanizing consequences of photographic voyeurism?" (109). For him, the answer is a resounding "yes." He warns readers against falling into the "emotional anaesthesia" portrayed in the book, by seeing Billy as an "artist-outlaw" figure (118). Perry Nodelman, on the other hand, cannot denounce photographic vision so completely, for he believes that "Billy's activities *are* identified with the methods of photography, and they might be a metaphor for the work of artists" (77). His solution lies in the distinction between Billy the Kid's photographic fixation and the photographic method of Michael Ondaatje. The latter, he argues, makes "things live and move in words, rather than simply to capture their image and stop them dead" (79).

Carrying Nodelman's ideas further, I would suggest that Michael Ondaatje's *Collected Works*, like "The Gate in His Head" and "King Kong Meets Wallace Stevens" (*Rat Jelly*), explores the idea that poetry can do both. Ondaatje, by looking at one extreme of the artistic impulse to fix and straitjacket reality, implicitly compares this method with his own fixing of Billy's character. As Stephen Scobie notes, comparing Ondaatje's Billy with that of bpNichol in *The True Eventual Story of Billy the Kid*: "Ondaatje's book *fixes* a certain view of the Kid into an intense, fully realized image," whereas Nichol's Billy is "insubstantial, flickering, changing, dying" ("Two Authors" 231). Perry Nodelman points out, too, that the essential character of Ondaatje's Billy is "static" and "unchanging" (69). Nevertheless, Ondaatje's use of several perspectives as well as several genres or media suggests that even a simple being – a man who has become a machine – may be viewed in a myriad of ways.

The use of actual photographs in *The Collected Works* emphasizes this necessary interplay between fixing Billy's story but not rendering it as a static artifact from the past. An early photograph of the interior of a log cabin is later reproduced – enlarged – so that the gun lying beside the bed is forced into prominence (45; 91). So, too, has Billy's mechanical nature been progressively brought into our range of vision. Another photograph, showing a man painting a sign, flanked by two walking men, with what appears to be the skeleton of an animal in the foreground, is a reminder that the role of the artist is not to dissect and analyse but to capture the subject in motion (13). Like the photograph of Robert Ross holding the skull of a rabbit, it may also suggest the all-important role of memory and the past.

Perry Nodelman's bewildered response to many of the photographs in *The Collected Works* may be accounted for in these same terms of fixity and motion, the past and the present. "[t]he people who do appear in later photographs seem incapable of the violence the book describes," he complains (68). Nodelman is probably thinking of the placid portrait of a man and a woman, calmly facing the camera, very likely meant to represent Sallie Chisum and Billy, since it faces on the opposite page Sallie's recollections of Billy (31). The photograph does, in fact, exploit the contrast between stasis and motion, forcing us to acknowledge the difference between notions of historical personages which have been fixed by the camera and the pen, and the raucous, lusty, chaotic experience which Ondaatje "fixes" for us, for example, in the episode of the night-long debauch at the Chisum ranch.

The photographic device which sums up this rejection of analysis and mechanical or historical fixity in the collection is the blank square above the opening words, *"I send you a picture . . . as quick as it can be worked."* Although this utterance has often been raised to the status of a definitive description of Ondaatje's collection, the words are undercut by the blank image above them. Any portrait of Billy, Ondaatje suggests, which demands fixity can only be incomplete, a blank portrait. Motion and flux, instead, must be captured by the fictional photographer. Therefore, the last photograph in *The Collected Works of Billy the Kid* – a small photograph of Ondaatje as a child, dressed in a cowboy outfit – is less a personal indictment, or a confession of destructive impulses, than a filling in of the blank rectangle which opened the collection. If analysis and dissection are futile tools in the search for Billy, Ondaatje presents the tool which is alone able to capture fixity-in-flux, life in the very act of being lived: the poet.

In *Coming Through Slaughter*, Ondaatje creates a portrait of another man caught up in the conflict between artistic fixity and flux, but this man is drawn to the former quality. Buddy Bolden, we are repeatedly told, is "almost completely governed by fears of certainty" (15); his music, rather, depends on the spontaneous and unexpected. Nevertheless, as the comment by clarinetist Frank Lewis suggests, Bolden may have been paradoxically "tormented by order, what was outside it" (37). Indeed, fixity and form are qualities which Bolden both "loathed and needed" (78). When he returns after a two-year absence to find Nora living with Willy Cornish, he experiences a "hunger to be as still as them . . . " (112).

Buddy's need for a spontaneity which does not exclude form places him at the opposite end of the spectrum not only from Billy the Kid, but from Webb, the detective who ultimately brings him back from musical obscurity only to force him over the brink of psychological obscurity. Webb is, as many readers have perceived, a representative of stifling fixity. It is, therefore, entirely appropriate that he should use the photograph as a forensic tool. "I need a picture" (50), he declares, and his need is by no means an aesthetic one. This association between photography and detective work is an old one; one thinks, for example, of Conan Doyle's articles for the *British Journal of Photography* ("With these *impedimenta* carefully corded up in a strong deal box," he assures us in "After Cormorants With a Camera," "I felt myself equal to any photographic emergency," [*Essays* 3]). In a similar vein, Webb finds himself running after a cornetist with a camera.

Webb is not the only detective, however, who hunts the mysterious, never-recorded jazz pioneer with a camera. As in Findley's *The Wars*, we witness a narrator-researcher who relies on interviews and photographs for information. Occasionally we are given these "data" directly, in a manner reminiscent of John Fowles's *The French Lieutenant's Woman* ("By the end of the Nineteenth Century, 2000 prostitutes were working regularly" [9]). More importantly, this researcher is a photographer himself, although, like Webb, he is less concerned with the aesthetic nature of his photographs than with their documentary value: "I easily hear the click of my camera as I take fast bad photographs into the sun aiming at the barber shop he probably worked in" (133). Ondaatje's researcher – like the mysterious figure who tosses a coin near the end of *The French Lieutenant's Woman* – represents the author, the maker of the fiction. Besides the fact that Ondaatje himself has taken photographs of such a barber shop, there is also the revealing comment:

When he went mad he was the same age
as I am now

The photograph moves and becomes a mirror. (133)

We are, therefore, persuaded that the conflict which Buddy feels within him, between form and shapelessness, is the same problem faced by the writer in assembling his book.

In *Coming Through Slaughter*, this conflict is captured in the close but mysterious relationship between Buddy and E.J. Bellocq – a photographer who did actually live and work in New Orleans at the turn of the century. "What could Buddy have to do with him?" (56), wonders Webb, and several critics of the novel have continued to wonder the same thing. An "unlikely friend," Roy MacSkimming christens Bellocq (92–94); and Ann Wilson, in her study of *Coming Through Slaughter*, admits that "[t]he basis of the friendship between Bolden and Bellocq is, at first, difficult to understand" (102). Even Buddy himself confesses that "[h]e didn't know how people like Bellocq thought. He didn't know how to put the pieces of him together" (125). Judging from one of Ondaatje's sources, a collection of Bellocq's photographs introduced by an interview, called *Storyville Portraits*, the mysteriousness of Bellocq's relationships with others is not a flaw in the novel, but a part of the Bellocq legend which Ondaatje has chosen to preserve. Johnny Wiggs, a New Orleans cornetist, responds to photographer Lee Friedlander's comment, "[t]he impression I've had is that nobody seems to really know Bellocq," by admitting that "he was awful hard to get to know" (Szarkowski 9). (The presence of a New Orleans cornetist in this interview leads one to believe that this interview may have been the genesis of Michael Ondaatje's decision to forge a close relationship between a photographer and a jazz musician who never actually knew each other.)

What ultimately brings Buddy and Bellocq together in Michael Ondaatje's work are the conflicts which they both face in their art. Surprising though it may seem, jazz and photography have been compared at some length by an American photography critic, A.D. Coleman:

Jazz . . . is the musical form whose philosophical basis is most akin to photography's. . . . In its rhythmic and harmonic attitudes, in its emphasis on intuition, spontaneity, and improvisation . . . jazz is directly linked to the idea of creativity as process consciousness, as *flow* in a Zen sense. (61-62)

Bellocq, like Buddy, finds it difficult to give this "intuition, spontaneity, and improvisation" a form. In reality, his photographs of New Orleans prostitutes did capture special, private moments in the drab lives of these women, yet in Ondaatje's work, he has trouble finding subjects, and an embarrassed Buddy must cajole the prostitutes into posing for him. Thus, Bellocq's question is the same question which haunts Buddy's music: how does one force that which must be spontaneous?

Bellocq's art is also similar to Buddy's in that it is closely allied with sexuality, as Stephen Scobie observes ("*Coming Through Slaughter*" 18). Bellocq's instructions to Buddy, while they are on their way to photograph the prostitutes, are full of *double entendres*: "But I don't want you there when I do it. . . . [J]ust introduce me and say what I want" (123). This last phrase is later echoed by Buddy just before he collapses: "What I wanted" (131). Buddy's playing is on this last occasion – as on others – associated with sexuality. During these last few minutes, he imagines his music getting caught in the hair of a "taunting" female figure in the audience. Earlier, Buddy presses his fingers on Robin's back "as though he were plunging them into a cornet" (59). Thus, art becomes another form of possession – a theme which Joseph Heller examined in *Catch-22* through the use of a photographer figure, Hungry Joe. Joe, a slapstick version of Bellocq, reflects of his photographic beauties: "[h]e could never decide whether to furgle them or photograph them, for he had found it impossible to do both simultaneously" (52). One is also reminded of films described by Susan Sontag in *On Photography*, such as Antonioni's *Blow-up*, which shows a fashion photographer simultaneously coveting his subject's body and clicking his camera, and Michael Powell's *Peeping Tom*, in which a madman, aided by a concealed weapon in his tripod, kills women while photographing them.

Although Bellocq and Buddy do not wish to destroy their

subjects or audience, they share a destructive impulse which finally turns inward. We first see Bellocq using his tripod as a weapon against Webb, pressing its three points against the body of the would-be intruder. Later, the camera on his back is likened to a "bow" (123). In a rage of frenzied impotence and voyeurism, Bellocq also slashes his photographs of women with his knife, "wanting to enter the photographs, to leave his trace on the bodies" (55). Ondaatje again transforms the legend of Bellocq for a particular reason; the speakers in *Storyville Portraits* speculate that it may have been Bellocq's brother, a priest, who scratched out the faces (not the torsos) on the plates rather than the photographs. For that matter, it may have been Bellocq himself, wishing to conceal the identities of several of his sitters. At any rate, Ondaatje has transformed the act into a more violent, destructive one, in order to show the paradoxical coexistence of voyeurism, destructiveness, and creativity in Bellocq:

> You can see that the care he took defiling the beauty he had forced in them was as precise and clean as his good hands which at night had developed the negatives. . . . The making and destroying coming from the same source, same lust, same surgery his brain was capable of. (55)

Bellocq's final work of creation is, ironically, his self-destruction. He places chairs all around him in a room measuring twenty feet by twenty feet – an ordered and framed photograph – sets fire to the room, and "falls, dissolving out of his pose" (67).

Buddy, too, is capable of both "[t]he making and destroying." Like Bellocq, whose developing acid spreads onto his hair, Buddy mingles creativity and destructiveness in his art. When he collapses during that final parade down Canal Street, his cornet must be pried away from *"the hard kiss"* of his lips – almost as though the musical instrument had sucked all of Buddy's life in a macabre kiss of death (131). This tie between Buddy and Bellocq is further strengthened by the description of Bellocq's death in *Storyville Portraits*:

He dropped right on Common and Carondelet ... he carried that Bantam Special. I'm positive he had that; I didn't see him, but I could almost bet that he had that Bantam Special on him when he fell. (Szarkowski 18)

Since Bellocq represents the type of artist who mingles creation and destruction, he is the object of much blame for Buddy's condition – both inside and outside the novel. "*Look at you. Look at what he did to you. Look at you. Look at you. Goddamit. Look at you*" (127), Nora furiously challenges Buddy, and Willy Cornish later comments that "I think Bellocq corrupted him with that mean silence" (145). Roy MacSkimming, reviewing the novel, agrees with Willy; Bellocq is the shadowy figure who "placed no value whatever on Bolden's music and made him mistrust his fame, feel its mocking emptiness" (94).

Like Alice Munro's shadowy photographer in *Lives of Girls and Women*, Ondaatje's Bellocq has been judged too harshly. Sam Solecki alone points out that Bellocq cannot be directly blamed for Bolden's madness, that "[w]ith or without Bellocq's influence Bolden would have destroyed himself. . . . Bellocq simply hastened the process by making Bolden self-conscious of the inherent contradiction in his situation," that is, the coexistence of creativity and destructiveness ("The Making and Destroying" 42). Like Munro's photographer, Bellocq, whose work is likened by Bolden to "windows" (59), provides a mordant commentary on what lies beneath the surface of human endeavours.

Beyond merely acquitting Bellocq on the grounds of non-responsibility, one may point out that Bellocq, even with his destructive impulses, is a more positive artist figure than Webb, for instance. To equate Bellocq and Webb, as Stephen Scobie does in calling them "the two extremes towards which he [Buddy] is drawn" minimizes enormous differences between them ("*Coming Through Slaughter*" 7). Bellocq is, in contrast to the non-aesthetic concerns of Webb and even of the researcher, a perfectionist; he prepares the photograph which Webb only wants to use for detective work in "a fussy clinical way" (52). In fact, Bellocq, unlike Webb, is not only aesthetically sensitive, but humanly sensitive as well. Buddy defends Bellocq against Nora's charges, calling his photographs "beautiful" and "gentle" (127). Indeed, the narrator takes great pains to point out the sensitivity of Bellocq's portraits of prostitutes – a sensitivity which seems all the more incredible when one realizes the initial unwillingness of his subjects. As in his relationship with Buddy, Bellocq waits for his subject to become "self-conscious," so that she "remembers for the first time in a long while the roads she imagined she could take as a child. And he photographed that" (54). Ondaatje is again building on the legend of Bellocq from *Storyville Portraits*; Lee Friedlander ponders, in a similar fashion: "It almost looks as if each girl decided what she wanted to be like . . . some of them wanted to be nude and some of them wanted to look like they were going to church. He just let them act out whatever they had in mind for themselves" (Szarkowski 15). This conception of the real Bellocq is borne out by Naomi Rosenblum, who comments that: "these arrangements of figure and decor project a melancholy languor that seems to emanate from both real compassion and a voyeuristic curiosity assuaged by the camera lens" (267). Of the fictional Bellocq's compassion, one has only the testimony of Buddy, who repeatedly calls him "dear Bellocq" and who significantly carries his frail friend up the stairs of the whorehouse, not wishing "to damage the camera or hurt the thin bones in the light body . . . " (126). The fragility of their lives and art brings Buddy and Bellocq together.

For all of his fragility, Bellocq is strongly antagonistic to Webb and his investigations. Although he supplies the detective with a photograph of Buddy and his band, he (like his photographs) conceals more than he reveals about Buddy and Nora. This protective concealment is perfectly summed up in his destruction of the negatives of the photographs of Buddy and Nora: "Goodbye. Hope he don't find you" (53). In this instance, destruction is a positive act, for it leaves Webb with nothing but a "damp picture in his hand" and an assortment of visual impressions of Bellocq which he scrupulously analyses (56-57). In the end Webb is carried further away from the essence of Buddy Bolden's life by his researches; Bellocq alone has access to that secret, inner world.

Bellocq also stands opposed to Webb in that he represents the flight away from the ravenous audience which threatens to devour the artist. Robert Kroetsch christens him "the photographer as version of artist. The photographer ignoring audience" (61). Bellocq is, of course, his own audience, taking photographs of the Storyville prostitutes for his own use, not prostituting himself to his audience, as Buddy does. "He was the first person I met," claims Bolden, "who had absolutely no interest in my music" (59) – a statement which is less a denunciation of Bellocq than a warm commendation. Bellocq, unlike Webb, does not seek to bring Buddy back from obscurity and thrust him before an audience. As Buddy says, "he tempted me out of the world of audiences where I had tried to catch everything thrown at me" (91). Bellocq prefers to allow Buddy to sink into obscurity and sanity, like the negatives slowly dissolving into whiteness in his tray.

Finally, Bellocq's art – like the photography in *Billy the Kid* – cannot be viewed as a purely destructive, fixed art, because, like Buddy's music, it serves as an analogue to Ondaatje's own art. In the photographs of Bellocq, as in *Coming Through Slaughter*, the past is mixed with the present, and fantasy is mixed with external fact: "What you see in his pictures is her mind jumping that far back to when she would dare to imagine the future ... " (54). This fluid temporal movement recalls the comments made by Timothy Findley and Alice Munro about the time sequence involved in reading and writing short stories. Compare, too, the discontinuous nature of Buddy's music: "I wanted them [the audience] to be able to come in where they pleased and leave when they pleased and somehow hear the germs of the start and all the possible endings at whatever point in the music that I had reached *then*" (94). Ondaatje's aim is precisely the same; as he commented to Sam Solecki, during the writing of *Coming Through Slaughter*: "what I'm doing doesn't have a preformed shape" ("Interview" 53). The short, sharply defined scenes and fragments of writing carry even further the brief, photographic style of Timothy Findley's prose; they emphasize that *Coming Through Slaughter* is both a series of images and a fluid dream-like prose poem. In this way, Ondaatje achieves once more an artistic truce between fixity and flux.

The most important example of this truce is Ondaatje's use of the photograph of Buddy and his band. Robert Kroetsch sees the static photograph as life-denying: "Posing. Posed. Poised. Silent. .... Photo: arrest. Killing. Going. The camera as weapon. With, but against, the novel" (61). I would argue that the image of the six musicians works with rather than against the novel. It appears either on or inside the cover of Ondaatje's book, like a talisman. Moreover, Ondaatje's translation of the visual image into linguistic terms thus:

Jimmy Johnson   Bolden   Willy Cornish   Willy Warner
on bass   on valve trombone   on clarinet

         Brock Mumford   Frank Lewis
         on guitar   on clarinet   (66)

is, in itself, a comment on the interdependence of the word and the image. In fact, many readers probably read the testimonies by the band members in the book, flip to the photograph key, and then to the photograph itself, to see the image behind the word – a fluid reading style which forms a perfect testimony to the complex interrelationships between the image and the word which Ondaatje has created in *Coming Through Slaughter*.

Running in the Family represents Michael Ondaatje's return to the land which he once christened the "unphotographed country," Sri Lanka. In this fictional journey into the forgotten, unexplored regions of Ondaatje's past, the photograph becomes a visual testament to memory, and to the continuity of the human family. In fact, the book is hybrid in form, at once memoir, fiction, and photograph album, like David Galloway's 1978 novel, *A Family Album*. Galloway uses the stages in the development of the modern camera as a metaphor for the passing on of succeeding generations in his family. In *Running in the Family*, memory, especially, surfaces in a way unequalled in any of Ondaatje's earlier work. The entire journey of rediscovery finds its genesis in an image: "those relations from my parents' generation who stood in my memory like frozen opera. I wanted to touch them into words" (*Running* 22). As in *Coming Through Slaughter*, therefore, Ondaatje feels an overwhelming desire to make image and word meet and create.

Memory, in fact, gives the memoir its shifting, dream-like quality. In *Running in the Family* particularly, Ondaatje seems fascinated by the complex workings of memory – especially by their similarity to storytelling. "Whether a memory or funny hideous scandal," he says of his family's discussions, "we will return to it an hour later and retell the story with additions . . . " (26). The chronology of the conventional memoir is indeed interrupted, made fluid; halfway through the book Ondaatje claims that his mother's sighting of a pair of *kabaragoyas* (monitor lizards) six months before his birth is his "first memory" (75). This ordered miscellany Ondaatje appropriately compares to a woven fabric, "each memory a wild thread in the sarong" (110).

His impulse to give random memory some order leads him to develop the same photographic vision which Del Jordan develops in *Lives of Girls and Women*. "My body must remember everything" (202), he tells himself on the morning of his departure from Sri Lanka, and we learn in the acknowledgement that he, like Del, and Gilbert Winslow in *The Last of the Crazy People*, has experienced a hunger for lists, "long lists of confused genealogies and rumour" (205). This hunger for precision quickly turns into a hunger for photographs. "I would love to photograph this," muses Ondaatje, surrounded by his storytelling aunts, before he proceeds to "photograph" it in words with penetrating yet delicate vision: "The thin muscle on the upper arms, the bones and veins at the wrist that almost become part of the discreet bangle, all disappearing into the river of bright sari or faded cotton print" (110).

If photographs allow us to fix the precious moment of the present, they are no less an entrée into the complex and often obscure world of the past. The photograph of Ondaatje's father as a young man "posing slyly in uniform" during a trip to Ireland to fight against "the Rebels" (about which most of his relatives knew nothing), offers a glimpse into a fascinating secret life (32). On a larger scale, historical events which have similarly escaped the notice of society's recorders are often disclosed to us by the ubiquitous camera. A long, random list of the events of 1932, the year of Ondaatje's parents' marriage, combines the earth-shattering with the unrecorded: "Charlie Chaplin was in Ceylon. He avoided all publicity and was only to be seen photographing and studying Kandyan dance" (38). Similarly, ten photographs of drawings done by a rebel during the insurgency represent "the only record of them" because they were washed away by a flood. "The artist," Ondaatje tells us, "is anonymous" (85), and yet he joins the ranks of artists such as Buddy Bolden, whose legends have lived on, even though their original works have not. The photograph, in short, allows us precious access to a history which was either not recorded or evanescent.

This ever-growing regard for photography's powers of preservation accompanies Ondaatje's increasing fascination with human interaction and continuity. "Truth disappears with history," claims Ondaatje, "and gossip tells us in the end nothing of personal relationships" (53). The image of the human pyramid which recurs throughout *Running in the Family* acts as a visual representation of this complex web of relations among human beings. In a dream-vision, for instance, he sees "my own straining body which stands shaped like a star and realize gradually I am part of a human pyramid," his family laughing and chattering as they move across the living room without breaking the human chain (27). Earlier, Ondaatje refers to the doors of that same family room as "twenty feet high, as if awaiting the day when a family of acrobats will walk from room to room, sideways, without dismantling themselves from each other's shoulders" (24). In Galloway's *A Family Album*, interestingly, one of the family photographs shows an uncle and various relatives sitting on a picnic table described as "a kind of clumsy, but highly serviceable wooden pyramid" (65). One is also reminded of James Reaney's visual use of this image in *Colours in the Dark* (1969).

In *Running in the Family*, the group portrait becomes the photographic symbol of this human pyramid. Aunt Dolly's memorable parting gesture to her nephew is her proud display of a group photograph, taken years ago, of herself, Ondaatje's irrepressible grandmother Lalla, and friends and family members dressed up for a fancy costume party (Fig. 5). "She has looked at it for years," her nephew realizes, and "laughs at the facial expressions she can no longer see. It has moved tangible, palpable, into her brain, the way memory invades the present in those who are old . . . " (112). The photograph thus preserves and enshrines the very texture and nuances of the "complex relationships" in his family in a way clearly analogous to the preservative power of memory (53). In addition, the "embrace" of the aunt and nephew at their parting is an extension of this group photograph – another visual sign of the close relationship between one family member and another, between the past and the present. Ondaatje, in his work, carries on the process of preserving and celebrating the past which his aunt, her sight diminishing, can no longer perform; his placing of the actual photograph at the beginning of this section, "Eclipse Plumage," is a testimony to the continuity of human life and legend.

Although *Running in the Family* celebrates this passing on of the human spirit to succeeding generations, it does not ignore the painful possibility of the loss of tradition or of icons. Homes in Sri Lanka are continually described as being invaded by the natural world, be it in the form of floods, snakes, or tiny "silverfish" which "slid into steamer trunks and photograph albums – eating their way through portraits and wedding pictures" (135–36). Ondaatje is clearly horrified by this loss of a recorded past. "What images of family life they consumed in their minute jaws and took into their bodies no thicker than the pages they ate," he wonders, aghast (136). The minute silverfish, like the infinitesimal passing seconds of time, have the awful power to obliterate whole generations. Ironically, at this point Ondaatje experiments with another form of recording his Sri Lankan surroundings which might be less subject to corrosion – the tape-recording of night-time noises. Although this record may rival or even better the camera in accuracy, it cannot touch the precious moments which Ondaatje celebrates in his fictional memoir: the moments of the past.

As the comparison between the tape-recorder and the camera suggests, the photograph's dominion over fact is not supreme. Photographs can deceive, just as the elaborate maps which cover the walls of Ondaatje's brother's house are "false maps" which are "growing from mythic shapes into eventual accuracy" (63). The group photograph of the Sinhalese cast of *Camelot*, taken in Sir John Kotelawala's garden, is a flagrant piece of deception, not unlike the actor's art: "Guinevere kisses Arthur beside the tank of Australian fish" (159). The exotic, dream-like setting of Sri Lanka, Ondaatje implies, needs no prompting from British utopias or photographic devices. Indeed, his host Sir John Kotelawala immediately recounts an example of the camera's power to deceive. A young man, hired by the opposition party, pretending to suck the venom from a "snake bite" on a woman's thigh, is actually creating the appearance of a sexual scene, in which the camera catches Sir John's apparent consent (159–60). Thus the camera, like a historical event, can be exploited to suit human ambition.

Beyond this political truth, one must also recognize that the dual nature of the photograph – as icon and as barefaced liar – comments on the very nature of Ondaatje's fictional biography. Photographs and maps of Sri Lanka which may or may not be true prepare us for the continually shifting, unsteady basis of this family history. "Wait a minute, wait a minute," Ondaatje as frustrated researcher interrupts a complex family story, "[w]hen did all this happen, I'm trying to get it straight" (105). The same compulsion leads his brother to urge him, "You must get this book right. ... You can only write it once" (201). In his attempt to "get it straight" and "right," Ondaatje turns to various means such as a tape-recorder and "compulsive questioning" (205), only to find that the past does not yield its secrets so easily. Of his father, he admits that "he is still one of those books we long to read whose pages remain uncut. We are still unwise" (200). He concludes: "In the end all your children move among the scattered acts and memories with no more clues" (201). Like Findley's intrepid researcher in *The Wars*, Ondaatje (and all of us) must work with fragments, the elusive corners of photographs.

Ondaatje comes to terms with this frustrating truth by tossing aside the objective of discovering unimpeachable fact and joyously embracing fabrication and distortion. In this very act, he carries on a family tradition; the tendency which he notes in his mother's generation, of "recording by exaggeration" (169). His closing note in the acknowledgements is therefore a serious statement of his artistic intent and his conscious following of family tradition in *Running in the Family*: "if those listed above disapprove of the fictional air I apologize and can only say that in Sri Lanka a well-told lie is worth a thousand facts" (206).

The all-encompassing image of this artistic truce between fact and fantasy is the photograph which Ondaatje tells us he has been "waiting for all my life" – a photograph of his parents, Mervyn and Doris Ondaatje, taken while they were on their honeymoon in 1932 (see fig. 6). This portrait, like his brother's maps, is a distortion, especially if one compares it with the handsome portraits of his parents which appear earlier in the memoir:

My father's pupils droop to the south-west corner of his sockets. His jaw falls and resettles into a groan that is half idiot, half shock.... My mother in white has twisted her lovely features and stuck out her jaw and upper lip so that her profile is in the posture of a monkey. The print is made into a postcard and sent through the mail to various friends. On the back my father has written "*What we think of married life.*" (161–62)

Nevertheless, this caricature is, in the eyes of their son, accurate and meaningful, what Alice Munro would call a "true lie." It provides, for Ondaatje, "[t]he evidence I wanted that they were absolutely perfect for each other," a conclusion which the factual evidence of their later divorce could not sustain. "It is the only photograph I have found of the two of them together," claims Ondaatje, and the image truly speaks of the human togetherness and saving humour of a marriage.

This photograph is a crucial discovery for Michael Ondaatje the artist and the son. Doris and Mervyn, with their facial contortions, reveal themselves to be "hams of a very superior sort" (162). The epithet could apply equally to the writer, who changes or distorts language to make human experience meaningful. Unlike the Sinhalese actors playing in *Camelot*, however, Ondaatje has used his powers of distortion to create a myth about his own land, Sri Lanka.

This belief that distortion tells a more meaningful truth than the local records office informs the entire conception of *Running in the Family* as well as *Coming Through Slaughter* and *The Collected Works of Billy the Kid*. As Ondaatje gradually discovers, photography can both fix our sense of truth and liberate it, by leading us not only into history but beyond history. If the maps of Ceylon from ancient to modern times take us "from mythic shapes into eventual accuracy" (*Running in the Family* 63), Michael Ondaatje's photographic fiction reverses the process, leading us from mere accuracy back into the compelling "mythic shapes" of our past.

Chapter Four

✠

" Today Facing Yesterday ":
Photography in Margaret
Laurence's Works

Photography and storytelling: these two arts which are so closely associated in Michael Ondaatje's works come together once more in the work of another photographic novelist, Margaret Laurence. Although Laurence is not as daring a formal experimenter as Ondaatje or Findley, the influence of photography and film has led her away from the more traditional narrative forms of *This Side Jordan* (1960) and *The Stone Angel* (1964) to more daring experiments in visual writing in *The Fire-Dwellers* (1969) and *The Diviners* (1974). What has remained constant in her fiction, however, is her use of the photograph to suggest the startling juxtaposition of past and present, whether in the lives of her Ghanaian or Somali characters, or in the lives of the citizens of Manawaka. In fact, a story which she relates in her collection of essays, *Heart of a Stranger* (1976), might act as the perfect summation of Margaret Laurence's conception of the photograph. While travelling in Greece, the Laurences were impressed by the archway at Olympia, through which the Olympic athletes ran, centuries ago, on their way to the arena. Jack Laurence's attempt to capture this haunting sense of an ancient place with his camera was foiled, however, by the intrusion of an unmistakeably twentieth-century teenager:

> I suggested that he take a picture anyway, with the denim-clad American boy walking into the ancient stadium – Today facing Yesterday. He agreed and

prepared to take his picture. At that precise moment the boy turned around. Today was facing Today, and they were both holding cameras aimed at each other. (27)

Margaret Laurence's works could indeed be construed as a series of confrontations between today and yesterday – confrontations which are communicated to us through retrospective narrative techniques in *The Stone Angel*, *The Fire-Dwellers*, and *The Diviners*. In addition, the humorous meeting of the two camera eyes in Laurence's anecdote might well represent her consciousness of each person's capacity to frame, capture, and interpret experience (or, as we shall see, fictionalize it). Stacey, Hagar, Morag, and Rachel are all cameras, "ever-open eyes," to borrow a phrase from *The Fire-Dwellers*, allowing Margaret Laurence to study human beings of today facing the burdens and joys of yesterday.

Margaret Laurence's responses to visual forms of communication differ greatly from those of Munro, Findley, and Ondaatje, in that hers are much more tentative. Although she is no stranger to visual art (her contact with African art is well documented in *Heart of a Stranger* [1976] and *The Prophet's Camel Bell* [1963]), she does not openly espouse common artistic aims with painters, sculptors, or photographers. Nevertheless, her prose has frequently been praised for its painterly qualities. Clara Thomas refers to Laurence as a writer who displays "a painter's sense of colour and composition" (*Margaret Laurence* 19), who creates "patterns of Chiaroscuro" (58). *The Fire-Dwellers* (Laurence's most visually daring novel) she likens to "a vast canvas by Hieronymus Bosch whose every corner is filled with devilish manifestations of aberration, cruelty, and desperation..." (*Manawaka World* 118). Similarly, George Woodcock applauds the "precise and brilliant brushwork" (*A Place to Stand On* 29) of *The Tomorrow-Tamer* (1963) and the "modulated" colours and "sombre tones" (31) of *A Bird in the House* (1970).

The subject of painting is by no means scarce in Laurence's fiction; the Ghanaian painter Danso in "The Merchant of Heaven" from *The Tomorrow-Tamer* paints the sights and people of his nation, even though he "knew it was not fashionable" (60). Here, painting is not only an aesthetic object, but a political act. Painting is equivalent to politics, too, for Dan McRaith, the Scottish painter who is Morag's lover in *The Diviners*. His canvas, *The Dispossessed*, which depicts "[a] grotesquerie of a woman, ragged plaid-shawled, eyes only unbelieving empty sockets, mouth open in a soundless cry ... and in the background, a burning croft" (309), speaks eloquently of Dan's native Scotland and of his own condition as one of the dispossessed in England. Painting, for Hagar Shipley, represents not political realism but what she calls "a measure of gracefulness in an ungainly world" (*Stone Angel* 62). The steel engraving of *The Death of General Wolfe* and the Holman Hunt knight and lady (probably his *Lady of Shalott*) present comfortingly sentimentalized portrayals of death and sex, respectively. Rosa Bonheur's *The Horse Fair*, as Bram Shipley crudely points out, allows Hagar to enjoy the horse without considering the manure (83). Therefore, although Laurence frequently refers to painting in her novels and stories, she is more interested in its political symbolism, or in its misuse, in its capacity to distance us from the earthy or elemental, than in its positive associations with her art.

Laurence feels, however, no qualms about discussing the visual aspects of her writing. "My writing has always tended to be visual," she told Graeme Gibson, "which is just partly my natural way of doing things" (186). The "natural" and the "visual" are often associated in Laurence's mind with her craft. In "Gadgetry or Growing: Form and Voice in the Novel," she explains her conception of form by using an elaborate metaphor which is both visual and natural:

> I have to put it in visual terms – I see it not like a house or a cathedral or any enclosing edifice, but rather as a forest, through which one can see outward, in which the shapes of trees do not prevent air and sun, and in which the trees themselves are growing structures, something alive. (81)

In fact, Laurence repeatedly sees structure in visual terms; speaking of *A Bird in the House* (a short-story collection which is a structural counterpart to Alice Munro's *Lives of Girls and*

Women and *Who Do You Think You Are?*), Laurence once again maintains that "the outlines of a novel . . . and those of a group of stories such as these interrelated ones may be approximately represented in visual terms." That is, a novel's themes and characters may be compared to wavy, interconnected horizontal lines, and those of an interconnected short-story collection to parallel vertical lines ("Time and the Narrative Voice" 157). It is no wonder that a writer who chose the form of *A Bird in the House* – a form which we have already likened to a series of snapshots in discussing Alice Munro's fiction – should then write a novel incorporating this structure: *The Diviners*, which opens with Morag Gunn carefully arranging a series of photographs from her childhood in chronological order.

This concern with visual form originates for Laurence, as for Findley and Ondaatje, primarily in her contact with film. "I think that every writer, in this particular time, in our age, has learned a great deal from both films and from TV" (186), she told Graeme Gibson, and she also characterized her writing to him in cinematic terms, confessing her difficulty in creating "a broad screen, as it were" (196). Certain passages from Laurence's work do tend to remain in one's memory in the form of filmed sequences on a screen: for example, Hagar's painful descent on the stairway at Shadow Point, or Christie Logan making grotesque faces to appease the teasing Manawaka children. A theatrical agent in New York made the same discovery while reading a review of *A Jest of God* (1966) in *Life* magazine – thus began the film version of the novel, entitled *Rachel, Rachel* (Hind-Smith 40). According to Marcienne Rocard, the cinematic quality of Laurence's novels is a result of consciously chosen narrative techniques: the careful orchestration of present tense, past tense, and third-person narration. The present tense, she argues: *"est le temps privilégié par les mass media"* ("is the favoured tense of the mass media") because it suggests immediacy (114). Moving back and forth from present to past, from today to yesterday, she therefore concludes, produces *"une vision stéréoscopique des choses"* ("a stereoscopic vision of things" [115]).

One qualifying consideration must be added to Rocard's detailed study of Laurence's cinematic style: Laurence's own fundamental scepticism about any strict analogy between fiction and film. Laurence, unlike Findley and Ondaatje, shies

124

away from any involvement in film-making; she sees that medium and her own as "totally different" (186) and screen-writing as an endeavour that she "wouldn't have touched ... with a ten-foot pole" (Gibson 188). While she acknowledges that she and other writers have imported certain narrative techniques from film, she maintains that the two media rule different domains, that there are some things "a film can do which I really can't do adequately in words. . . . But on the other hand, there isn't any way that a film can catch the inner workings of the individual brain in the way that a novel can" (Gibson 187). Film is, for Laurence, both a nourisher and a source of anxiety; she believes that novelists "have to concentrate on things that film cannot do" (Gibson 186–87), just as late nineteenth- and early twentieth-century realist painters feared that photography was robbing them of the traditional mimesis handed down to them from seventeenth-century Dutch painting. Laurence, like the impressionists and the later abstractionists, seeks refuge from the camera in psychology.

Part of the reason for Laurence's unwillingness to move freely from film to word (as Michael Ondaatje does, for instance, in *Sons of Captain Poetry*) is her perception of film as a popular, less serious genre. She is clearly pained (with some reason) by an Englishwoman's introduction of her at a party as the woman who "wrote the book of *Rachel, Rachel*, and *just think* – I knew it when it was *only a novel!*" Her daughter's ecstatic greeting of the newspaper articles about the film ("Fame at last!" [Hind-Smith 41]), elicits a similarly wry response. "As much as I was interested in the film," Laurence maintains, "to me it is *still* only a novel" ("Gadgetry or Growing" 86). Laurence is also well aware of the political dangers of film and television – the tendency to distance the viewer from atrocities and injustices which Susan Sontag has noted. In a convocation address, she attacked the glittering media world of the nuclear arms race. "Do the world's leaders really suppose that it would all happen on TV, and that the dead would get up again and take on a different role in another popular series so they might be killed again and again?" she demanded ("A Statement of Faith" 57).

A major reason for this cautious view of photography and fiction is, I would argue, Laurence's insistence on the primacy of the word. Clara Thomas felt that film would be the perfect medium for *A Jest of God*, since "[t]he camera will, naturally, supply the distance, the other focus, that the words do not always afford," referring, one assumes, to the inward-turning nature of the novel (*Margaret Laurence* 53). Laurence, however, disagreed. For her, film could not do justice to the complex thoughts of Rachel Cameron precisely because "they couldn't have interminable voice-over" (Gibson 186). It is significant that Laurence should think of the voice-over as the nearest one could come to reproducing the words of her novel. Unfortunately, voice-overs, used often when a film is based on a novel, can have disastrous effects on the visual production. Film-makers tend to use them sparingly, perhaps only at the beginning or end of a film, to suggest another level of narration. As Thomas guessed, the film-makers relied primarily on visual clues in *Rachel, Rachel*, particularly the gestures and facial expressions of the actress.

More importantly, words for Laurence are powerful totems which have a solidity and permanence which visual images alone lack. For instance, Morag, when she receives the Currie plaid pin in a trade with Jules Tonnerre, must immediately turn to words in order to give this visual icon meaning; she goes "to her bookshelves and gets out Christie's *The Clans and Tartans of Scotland*" (352). She also sees the act of naming visual objects, such as Catharine Parr Traill's naming of flowers, as an act of power: "Like the Garden of Eden. Power! Ecstasy! I christen thee Butter-and-Eggs!" (138). As the reference to the garden of Eden suggests, Laurence's feeling of "respect for words" (Gibson 185) largely grows out of her adoption of the Bible as an analogue to and source of her own stories. As Laurence herself declares in *Heart of a Stranger*, "I have had, if any faith at all, a faith in the word. *In the beginning was the Word, and the Word was with God, and the Word was God*" (203).

Even when Laurence deals with the conflict between oral and written communication, the word emerges supreme and inescapable. Her translations of Somali legends and poetry, *A Tree for Poverty* (1953), prepare the way for her later study of verbal and oral storytelling in *The Diviners*. As W.H. New has observed: "Repeatedly Laurence's method makes the oral forms of tale and proverb into observer's documents [One thinks here of the tape transcripts which are printed in *The Wars*], making saying into seeing . . . " ("The Other and I" 118). Words are, for

Morag, as they were for a younger Margaret Laurence in Somaliland, a way of fixing and preserving the tales of our ancestors. She marvels at the way in which Jules and Pique (both, appropriately, songwriters) communicate without the use of her precious words:

How unlike me. I would have had to say what I thought about it, analyze the words, probably, yakkity yak. She doesn't have to, and neither does Jules. They do it in a different way, a way I can see, although it's not mine. (348)

Nor is it Margaret Laurence's way; she once described herself as "an inveterate letter writer," whose typewriter is at the centre of her world, "a kind of radio transmitter" (*Heart of a Stranger* 198). How appropriate it is that *The Diviners* should close with Laurence's novelist-protagonist quietly returning to her house, "to write the remaining private and fictional words, and to set down her title" (370).

What Laurence has attempted to do, of course, is to capture the immediacy of Somali folk tales, of Métis song, of sensory experience of any sort, through verbal description, and for this reason her work has been termed realistic. As Laurence once commented in a letter to Clara Thomas: "one would like to convey a feeling of flesh-and-blood immediacy. . . . Which is not possible to convey, really, as art is never life . . ." (*Margaret Laurence* 10). Thomas herself associates this mimetic impulse with photography, claiming, for instance, that Laurence captures the world of Vanessa MacLeod through "a technique of double exposures" (*Manawaka World* 104). Yet photography for Margaret Laurence means much more than a scrupulous recording of detail. If one looks carefully at her handling of the photographic image from the early African fiction to *The Diviners*, one finds the same association of photography with the past, modern commercialism, human memory, and the fixity and flux of experience, which ones finds at various times in the works of Alice Munro, Timothy Findley, and Michael Ondaatje – even though the associations which Laurence makes may differ enormously in nature.

The Prophet's Camel Bell, Margaret Laurence's account of her stay in Somaliland, though published three years after *This Side Jordan*, is an indispensable guide to all of Margaret Laurence's African fiction. In relation to photography, in particular, the memoir establishes certain associations with vision and photographic vision which resurface in the fictional lives of Nathaniel Amegbe in *This Side Jordan*, and Danso and Godman in *The Tomorrow-Tamer*. Vision itself is a major feature of Laurence's account, as it is in travel books from Norman Douglas to the indispensable Baedeker. This passage, from the opening pages of *The Prophet's Camel Bell*, is a case in point:

> The Mediterranean, that time of year, was truly the wine-dark sea. High up on the *Tigre*, whipped by the icy wind, *we watched* the wild hills of Sicily pass by. At night *we saw* a far-off red glow. . . . And sometimes in the darkness *we saw* a phosphorescence. . . . (7; emphasis added)

Seeing is, indeed, a constant motif, yet the seeing eyes here are undoubtedly Western eyes. The reference to the wine-dark sea from Homer invokes the entire Western literary tradition – a tradition which leaves untouched the Muslims whom Laurence would later meet in Somaliland.

Throughout the memoir, this hint of the insufficiency of Western vision is fleshed out in explicit, dramatic situations. After Laurence commits her first act of indiscretion in Somaliland, walking alone on foot to a nearby Somali town, she tries to believe that she, as a well-meaning European, would be immune from attack by villagers who resent the European presence in Africa. "But they looked at me from their own eyes, not mine," she finally acknowledges (25). Much later, when she distributes quinine to local tribesmen, Laurence is frustrated to learn that some of them treat the pills like amulets, to be possessed or worn to ward off disease. "We were looking at the same object, the tribesmen and I, this vial of red tablets," she realizes. "But I suspect that we were not seeing the same thing." Laurence quickly adds that the Somalis were hardly deficient in observation; in the nineteenth century, they alone believed that malaria was caused by mosquitoes, while visiting English sahibs confidently ascribed the cause of the dreaded disease to putrid swamp fumes (81).

This contrast between Eastern and Western seeing informs Laurence's treatment of the visual arts and photography in particular. The Somalis, as Laurence notes, are discouraged as Muslims from making images, and, in addition, the country is "lacking in almost all materials needed for painting or sculpture" (190). Nevertheless, a young Somali teacher who comes to visit Laurence brings along a folder of some of his own paintings, "birds and twisting trees and flowers that looked as though they had been delicately transplanted from some Persian tapestry." Instead of appreciating the paintings as eloquent records of Eastern culture, however, an inexperienced Laurence immediately launches into private, embarrassing questions: "What did the Somali bride-price actually involve? . . . Did the clitoridectomy make it impossible for Somali women to enjoy sex?. . . . All at once, the brash tone of my voice was conveyed to my own ears, and I was appalled" (36). Here is one instance, at least, of where visual intuition might afford more knowledge and true understanding than verbal interrogation.

The visual form which is most clearly associated in *The Prophet's Camel Bell* with Western intrusion and insensitivity is the photograph. On the first page of her memoir Laurence captures the ebullient confidence of the Western traveller: "There you go, rejoicing, as so you should, for anything might happen and you are carrying with you your notebook and camera so you may catch vast and elusive life in a word and a snapshot" (1) – a telling conjunction of objects, in the light of our discussion of the word and the image in Margaret Laurence's eyes.

The photograph later becomes the visual equivalent of the insensitive questions which Laurence asks her bewildered and embarrassed visitors, for it, too, does not respect privacy. This time, the attractive nine-month-old son of the school gardener is Laurence's object of study:

> I decided to take his picture one day, as he sat on the ground, so placidly, sifting the dust through his fingers. I brought out my camera, but Ibrahim's mother hastily picked him up and covered his nakedness with her

headscarf. No Muslim man, however small, her re-
proachful glance seemed to say, could possibly be
peered at through the camera's eye when insufficiently
clothed. (44)

The taking of a photograph thus becomes an act of Western
aggression – a view not unlike that of Susan Sontag, who claims
that "[t]o photograph is to appropriate the thing photographed.
It means putting oneself into a certain relation to the world that
feels like knowledge – and, therefore, like power" (*On Photography* 4).

Laurence, let it be said, is no aggressor, yet for her the
desire to gain knowledge of Somali customs, to take photographs, is no doubt linked to feelings of disorientation in a new
place. As Sontag notes of tourist photography, in terms which
could easily relate to colonialism, "photographs . . . help people
to take possession of space in which they are insecure" (*On
Photography* 9). In Laurence's case, insecurity derives from the
knowledge that in Africa she represents, by virtue of her skin
colour, the oppressor. Similarly, Paul Fussell, in his study of
British literary travel between the wars, argues that the passport
photograph itself is subtly linked to feelings of embarrassment
and guilt on the part of the tourist:

So small a phenomenon as the passport picture is an
example of something tiny which has powerfully affected the modern sensibility, assisting that anxious
self-awareness, that secret but overriding self-contempt,
which we recognize as attaching uniquely to the world
of Prufrock and Joseph K. and Malone. (26)

Although Fussell does not trace these feelings of "self-awareness" and "self-contempt" to colonialism, it is certainly argu-
able that more than the human tendency to shrink from replicas
of oneself is involved. Does not the passport photograph clearly
announce a person's status as a traveller, isolating him or her as
an intruder, a stranger in a strange land?

In *The Prophet's Camel Bell*, photography is an even more
blatant sign of the Western exploitation of Africa. At Port Said,
a huckster selling cameras and other Western trinkets is heard
to exclaim, "Working for the Yankee dollah!" (8). More subtle is

130

Laurence's use of photography to comment upon the lives of Europeans living in Africa – especially the isolated community of Italians in Somaliland. Gino, one of Jack Laurence's foremen, takes great pains to show the Laurences "a picture of his wife when she was young and pretty." She was "growing old now, as he was, and they had been together very little" (149). Juxtaposed with this photographic symbol of exile and the homeland is the photograph which adorns the Italian Club at Hargeisa, "a framed picture of a blonde glamour girl" – a symbol of Western beauty (146). The two photographs together suggest the split consciousness of the European settler in Africa; nostalgia for the homeland on one hand, and a crude Western exploitativeness on the other. Indeed, the important links between photography and colonialism in *The Prophet's Camel Bell* prepare us for the fictional worlds of *This Side Jordan* and *The Tomorrow-Tamer*. The photograph in Laurence's African works powerfully suggests that the past presence of the white colonizers can be neither ignored nor erased.

In *This Side Jordan*, Laurence's first published novel, the first meeting between the colonizers and the colonized occurs, interestingly, at an exhibition of Ghanaian art. The clash between Miranda and Johnnie Kestoe and Nathaniel Amegbe, however, is only superficially related to art: "Of course, Nathaniel realized, the European thought he liked the picture only because it had been painted by an African" (41). Miranda, as well-intentioned and innocent as her Shakespearian counterpart, fumbles in her attempts to appear a concerned, liberal Westerner – sounding instead pitying and condescending:

> I think these exhibitions are a good idea. . . . It must do something to encourage African artists. There aren't many yet, are there? Of course, it's no wonder. The early missions must have done a great deal to wipe out indigenous art here. By forbidding image-making, I mean.

Nathaniel, for his part, reacts defensively to Miranda's well-meaning blunder:

'The missions tried to destroy our African culture – '

He stopped abruptly. He had overstated the case, overstated it deliberately. (42)

This entire conversational dance of defensiveness and guilt recalls a similar exchange over visual art described by Laurence in an essay in *Heart of a Stranger*, entitled, appropriately, "The Very Best Intentions." While Laurence was in Ghana, she consciously set about acquiring a liking for African art. Her proud display of a carved ebony bust to a Ghanaian produced a sharp exchange very similar to that between Amegbe and the Kestoes in *This Side Jordan*:

'Look – isn't this terrific? It's wonderful to see that carving is still flourishing in West Africa.'

Mensah laughed disdainfully. 'That? It's trash. They grind them out by the thousands. Europeans like that sort of thing, I suppose.'

Both of us were exaggerating, trying to make some planned effect. (35)

Whereas painting in *This Side Jordan* is associated with indigenous culture and the past, photography, as in *The Prophet's Camel Bell*, is exclusively a part of the Western tradition. Photography, like the sterile hospital, is part of the Western consciousness in which Nathaniel Amegbe is trying to take part. Nathaniel's Uncle Adjei, one of a series of family members who arrive on Nathaniel's doorstep to persuade him to let his wife Aya give birth at home, is puzzled by the modern furnishings of Nathaniel's home – not least by the "pictorial calendar whose message 'Happy New Year from Mandiram's The Quality Shop' was mysterious to him" (98). To the old tribesman, the commercial photograph, like the hospital, is artificial, removing the viewer, just as the hospital removes the patient, from the true sensations and experiences of life. Nathaniel, however, cannot adopt such a view; picture calendars and modernized hospitals are as undeniably a part of his life as the photograph of Daphne Manners is of Hari Kumar's in Paul Scott's *Raj Quartet* (Part 4, 1975).

The Tomorrow-Tamer carries even further this contrast between painting and photography. The narrator of the first story in the collection, "The Drummer of All the World," whose minister-father "forbade the making of wooden figures," reflects, like Miranda Kestoe, on the detrimental effects of Western religion on the African visual arts:

> "I suppose we have to thank men like my father for the sad fact that there are so few carvers of any merit left in West Africa.
> He broke idols literally as well as symbolically." (6)

The Muslim law forbidding graven images, Laurence implies, is at least an indigenous law; it is not a law forced on flourishing visual cultures, as is the corresponding Christian law.

Painting, therefore, becomes a powerful political tool for resisting the forces of Western culture in *The Tomorrow-Tamer* – a protest against the century-long attempt of the colonizers to eliminate it as a secular, pagan practice. In "The Merchant of Heaven," Danso, a painter of "mercurial energy," fights to bring his sensual, life-celebrating painting into the church of the sourly puritanical Brother Lemon. Fearing that the narrator's prediction that Brother Lemon will decorate the church with "[f]our-tone prints, done on glossy paper" (53) will come true, Danso gives voice to the naturalistic – and nationalistic – vision of his canvas:

> St. Augustine is on the river bank, see, the Congo or maybe the Niger. Bush all around. Ferns thick as a woman's hair. Palms – great big feathery palms. But very stiff, very stylized – Rousseau stuff. . . . And in the river . . . is the congregation, only they're hippos, see – enormous fat ones, all bulging eyes, and they're singing "Hallelujah" like the angels themselves, while old St. Augustine leads them to paradise. (54)

Danso is a modern African descendant of Browning's "Fra Lippo Lippi," whose secular versions of biblical scenes appear no less shocking than singing hippos to the ecclesiastical authorities:

Your business is not to catch men with show,
With homage to the perishable clay,
But lift them over it, ignore it all,
Make them forget there's such a thing as flesh. (206)

The confrontation between Danso and Brother Lemon is remarkably similar; Lemon hears of the planned hippo painting,
now transformed in Danso's mind into a throne of heaven, like
Lippi's ambitious project of painting "God in the midst,
Madonna and her babe, / Ringed by a bowery, flowery
angel-brood" (209–10), and asks, stunned: "You? . . . To paint
the throne of heaven?" (64).

Brother Lemon, it need hardly be said, is not the type of
churchman who can easily reconcile Rousseau and Raphael. In
fact, he is consistently associated by Laurence with photography rather than painting, and thus with Western influences. We
first see Brother Lemon on his arrival at the airport, confronting
his mission with the aid of two pieces of equipment: a water
purifier and a camera and projector kit. The water purifier sums
up perfectly and sardonically Brother Lemon's conception of his
charges; as the narrator marvels: "Suddenly I saw Brother
Lemon as a kind of soul-purifier, sucking in the septic souls and
spewing them back one hundred per cent pure" (53). The
camera performs a similar function in relation to the new land.
As Susan Sontag has argued, the camera allows us to put
distance between ourselves and the perceived object. Seen in
this way, Brother Lemon's camera allows him to distance
himself from the country he is facing; it becomes, in effect, a
reality purifier.

Brother Lemon's photography and Danso's painting represent polar opposites in "The Merchant of Heaven" – the West
and the East, the religious and the secular, the narrowly realistic
and the fictional or fantastic. When the narrator surveys one of
Danso's market scenes, he reflects that, in years to come, such
canvases will preserve the African culture which is now being
decimated by "hygienic skyscrapers" and "pidgin English"
(61). Brother Lemon, however, prefers the present as reflected
faithfully back to him via the camera lens; he dismisses Danso's
painting with hardly a comment and offers to show his assem-
bly-line battery of six rolls of slides. Danso's furious response:
"Every church needs pictures" (62), closely resembles Frey-

burg's "[e]verybody needs photographs" in *Famous Last Words* (390); in both instances, human beings are in danger of losing the past, or ignoring its relevance to the present.

The painting which Danso finally produces for the church proves the justice of the claim that everybody needs pictures. The canvas, "a picture of the Nazarene," reveals not the traditional "emaciated mauve-veined ever sorrowful Jesus" of bad religious art, but an ordinary man with "the body of a fisherman or a carpenter" (appropriately enough), "strong wrists and arms," and eyes which are "capable of laughter." Most importantly, he is shown surrounded by "a group of beggars, sore-fouled, their mouths twisted in perpetual leers of pain" (76) – the type of company which Brother Lemon's "reality purifier" would be sure to eliminate. This portrait, with its sober realism yet imaginative vision, represents the inspired joining of photographic realism with aesthetic and personal sensitivity. It is, in fact, a virtual counterpart to Fra Lippo Lippi's passionate depictions of "every sort of monk, the black and white . . . fat and lean," "good old gossips," and

> . . . the breathless fellow at the altar-foot,
> Fresh from his murder, safe and sitting there
> With the little children round him in a row
> Of admiration . . . . (211)

Danso has discovered the type of photographic seeing which does not distance the perceiver from the object, and which reveals, as does Alice Munro's fiction, the beauty invested in the unprepossessing and mundane. For Margaret Laurence, photographic vision includes the beautification of the mundane and a celebration of one's past, ideas which one finds stated most movingly by Browning's photographic realist of the renaissance, Fra Lippo Lippi:

> . . . we're made so that we love
> First when we see them painted, things we have passed
> Perhaps a hundred times nor cared to see;
> And so they are better, painted – better to us,
> Which is the same thing. . . . (37)

Margaret Laurence reveals a new respect for the photographic image in her Manawaka novels, precisely because it comes to express for her the same respect for the mundane and the cultural past which Danso's painting expresses in "The Merchant of Heaven." As a tool for rediscovering one's own cultural past instead of foisting the technological present upon another society, the photograph gains a new dimension in her eyes, a new capacity to reconcile past and present. For this reason, Laurence begins, in the late 1960s, to experiment with the photograph as an analogue to her narrative technique, which characteristically seeks to combine past and present experience.

Laurence's collection of essays, *Heart of a Stranger*, breathes the very spirit of the Manawaka novels (even though the collection includes three earlier African essays). Meditations on her own cultural heritage, such as "Man of Our People" (an admiring portrait of Gabriel Dumont) and "Road from the Isles," form a non-fictional parallel to the experiences of Morag and Hagar which is as striking as that between *The Prophet's Camel Bell* and the African fiction. More specifically, the essays reflect Laurence's growing obsession with her cultural past along with the acceptance of the photograph as a part of that cultural past. In a headnote to "Where the World Began," Laurence notes with surprise that she hadn't realized before collecting these essays that she had written so much on the theme of "the meaning to oneself of the ancestors ... before I ever dealt with it fictionally" (213).

Not only is this theme common to both her fiction and her non-fiction, but so is her manner of expressing it through visual images. In "Road from the Isles," Laurence recalls that her family "possessed certain trophies from the past, which I used to handle with curiosity and reverence, as though they had been religious relics" (146). One of these is a silver plaid pin with the Wemyss crest – an object which is veritably raised to the status of a "religious relic" by Hagar and, years later, by Morag. In the same essay, Laurence explains this curious hold of the visual past on her by dividing history into two categories: the intuitive understanding of our ancestors which we gain by visiting the ancestral homeland, and the more powerful kind of history, where simply "the names or tunes or trees ... can recall a thousand images ..." (157). As Morag discovers, the Currie plaid pin and Christie's book *The Clans and Tartans of Scotland* ultimately tell her more about herself than does visiting present-day Culloden, because those icons speak of the harsh struggle to keep cultural pride alive in a new land. It is hardly surprising, therefore, that Laurence's renewed fascination with the cultural icons of her homeland should include a fascination with one of the most ubiquitous of family icons: the photograph.

Another factor in Laurence's renewed interest in visual icons which cannot be ignored is her return, like Morag Gunn's, to the country of her birth. There Laurence evidently came to realize the profound visual effect which her homeland exerted and continued to exert on her sensibility. Of her prairie childhood she wrote in 1971: "Because that settlement and that land were my first and for many years my only real knowledge of this planet, in some profound way they remain my world, my way of viewing. My eyes were formed there" (213). Her contact with an entirely different visual environment in Ontario provoked further thoughts about the relationship between the visual world and words. "Words won't make a net to catch that picture," she writes of the flaming autumn forests near Bancroft. Still, she cannot resist adding: "I could see why the Group of Seven was so obsessed with trying to get it down ... and why, for so long, many Canadian writers couldn't see the people for the trees" (160). Appropriately, Laurence's own description of her life in Lakefield combines both visual and verbal activities: "writing, bird-watching, river-watching" (188).

Along with this visual renaissance, *Heart of a Stranger* bears witness to Laurence's changing attitudes toward the photographic icon. In her travel articles from Greece and Egypt, the photograph remains the symbol of Western commercialism that it is in her African fiction. A tour guide in Greece reduces Mount Parnassus to the status of something that "would make a terrific picture": " 'Come on, camera fans,' he croaked in his cheerful frog voice. 'All out!' " (22). As Susan Sontag humorously remarks: "Travel becomes a strategy for accumulating photographs" (*On Photography* 9). At Delphi, a capering madman with a camera leaps out from the columns of the temple, like "one of those mad seers or idiot shepherds who were always descending on the city in Greek plays and telling people things about themselves ..." (23–24). The camera, however, proves to be no tool for soothsaying; Laurence notes with evident disappointment that the capering madman is "only a commercial photographer" (24). The perfect image of the bizarre meeting of the camera and the ancient Greek empire is the hilarious moment when "Mrs. Takamura took a picture of her husband posing in the stadium as a discus thrower" – today facing yesterday, indeed (28).

Photography does, however, begin to suggest the cultural past as well as the vulgar present in several of the essays in *Heart of a Stranger*. Writing about the building of the Suez Canal, Laurence suddenly pauses to describe in full detail the present headquarters of the Suez Canal Authority in Ismailia. Although most of the headquarters belongs to "the world of right-this-minute," the room of de Lesseps, one of the pioneers of the canal, remains as it was a century ago, "a cadaver of the past." Prominent among the preserved relics is "a stilted photograph of de Lesseps and companions looking at once foolish and formidable in Bedouin dress." As Laurence notes, "[t]he dusty sense of a long yesterday is almost choking in here ..." (119). One thinks of the odd location of Juliet D'Orsey's apartments, full of photographs and memories, just above the inhumanly efficient Ministry of Scientific Information, in *The Wars*.

As in *Running in the Family* and *The Last of the Crazy People*, the family portrait in particular becomes an entrée into the shadowy world of the past in these essays. Writing of her childhood in Neepawa, Laurence says:

> The dead lived in that place, too. Not only the grand-parents who had, in local parlance, "passed on" and who gloomed, bearded or bonneted, from the sepia photographs in old albums, but also the uncles, forever eighteen or nineteen, whose names were carved on the granite family stones in the cemetery, but whose bones lay in France. (217)

This parallel between sepia-toned photographs and gravestones calls to mind the photograph of the serviceman John Harris in *The Last of the Crazy People*, placed carefully next to the box containing his revolver. As it does for Findley, the photograph becomes more and more in Laurence's eyes the perfect means of juxtaposing the past and the "right- this-minute."

✦ The Stone Angel (1964) ✦

One could think of no better description of the narrative method of <i>The Stone Angel</i> than the juxtaposition of the past and the "right-this-minute." The figure of the ninety-year-old "rampant with memory" Hagar Shipley, looking at her gallery of photographs, could well serve as an emblem of the entire novel. Indeed, these photographs, along with the objects in her Vancouver home, such as the glass decanter given to her as a wedding gift by Bram, and the oaken chair of Jason Currie, are Hagar's totems. "If I am not somehow contained in them and in this house, something of all change caught and fixed here, eternal enough for my purposes," she muses, "then I do not know where I am to be found at all" (36). This emphasis on catching and fixing change suggests the image of the photograph itself, as it does so powerfully at the end of Alice Munro's <i>Something I've Been Meaning to Tell You</i>: "Now I look at what I have done and it is like a series of snapshots. . . " (246).

More importantly, however, Hagar and her visual totems carry on the tradition of Jason Currie, whose monument to fixity and rigidity haunts the entire novel: "Above the town, on the hill brow, the stone angel used to stand . . . . my mother's angel that my father bought in pride to mark her bones and proclaim his dynasty, as he fancied, forever and a day" (3). For Hagar, too, visual artifacts are invested with all of the spiritual pride of her own dynasty. We see her repeatedly giving objects to her descendants: the Currie plaid pin to John, her mother's sapphire ring to Doris for Tina. Even Hagar herself becomes an artifact, a well-groomed example of dynastic sophistication and polish. "You're a credit to me" observes Jason Currie when Hagar arrives (43), newly polished and refined from the "young ladies' academy in Toronto" (42), and from that time on, Hagar makes sure that she is a credit to herself. "I wore the dusky rose silk suit I'd bought on sale that spring, and hat to match," recalls Hagar of the day she visited Lottie Dreiser in order to safeguard the inheritor of her dynasty, John. "Lottie seemed

139

quite stunned to see me looking so smart" (210).

Visual art, too, becomes for Hagar a means of exerting her superiority over others. At the same meeting with Lottie, Hagar notes with gleeful malice the aesthetic hodgepodge of the Simmons household: "A pleasant water color of the Bridge of Sighs was flanked by two plaster-of-Paris fishes," while "[a] Royal Doulton flower girl shared a wall shelf with a pink china poodle, the kind the five-and-ten stores sell . . . " (209). Hagar's well-groomed visual sophistication also brings her into sharp conflict with her husband, Bram, whose feeling for the Bridge of Sighs and fine china is less than enthusiastic. Hagar's admiration of Rosa Bonheur's *The Horse Fair* draws Bram's fury: "You never gave a damn for living horses, Hagar. . . . But when you see them put onto paper where they couldn't drop manure, then it's dandy, eh?" (83).

This aesthetic debate between realism and idealism (for behind Bram's vulgarity lies a particular view of art and life) is closely linked to the role of photography in the novel. Hagar's disposal of her Holman Hunt knight and lady "playing at passion" (83) comes hard upon the heels of her gloomy recognition that Bram is no Sir Galahad. (One might compare Rose's rejection of the similarly melodramatic Burne-Jones painting *The Beggar Maid* in Alice Munro's story of the same title.) Juxtaposed with the memory of this artistic disenchantment, however, is the incident in the present of Hagar scrutinizing the two paintings hanging in Dr. Corby's waiting room:

> One is a lake and thin poplar trees, the blues and greens merging and blending. . . . It reminds me of the spring around home. . . .
>
> I stand up and look closer. Whoever painted that picture knew what he was about. The other's one of those weird ones, the kind Tina professes to like, all red and black triangles and blobs that make no sort of sense. (82)

Hagar has, unexpectedly, become a champion of realism, of Constable over Miró. She regards the landscape painting as one might regard a photograph, relating it primarily to the past, and to objects or scenes which have been actually visualized; familiar, not idealized or conceptualized like the Holman Hunt print, the engraving of *The Death of General Wolfe*, and the abstract painting. One could describe this radical transformation of Hagar's vision by altering the famous description of Anne Elliot in Jane Austen's *Persuasion*: Hagar forces herself into romance in her youth, and learns realism as she grows older. Hers, too, is a "natural sequel of an unnatural beginning" (58).

The photograph provides, as one would expect, a model for Hagar's renewed interest in realism and the past. As a young married woman, Hagar seeks comfort in the images of "gauzy ladies performing Chopin in concert halls, proven by photographs to exist somewhere" (126). Photographs are, on a literal level, incontrovertible proof that something exists. One thinks, for example, of the photograph as irrefutable proof even for Sherlock Holmes in Conan Doyle's "A Scandal in Bohemia." During his conversation with the King of Bohemia, Holmes asks:

'If this young person should produce her letters for blackmailing or other purposes, how is she to prove their authenticity?'
'There is the writing.'
'Pooh, pooh! Forgery.'
'My private note-paper.'
'Stolen.'
'My own seal.'
'Imitated.'
'My photograph.'
'Bought.'
'We were both in the photograph.'
'Oh, dear! That is very bad!' (23)

Similarly, photographs provide validation for Hagar – reassurance that, even in the ramshackle Shipley house, cultured ladies playing Chopin can be as palpable a reality as the dirty kitchen linoleum tiles. (Hagar's cultured photographs are juxtaposed with Bram's reading material, "the catalogues from Eaton's and The Hudson's Bay" whose photographs depict objects probably closer in nature to linoleum tiles [125].)

An older Hagar turns to photographs to provide herself with validation of an entirely different nature; validation of the past and of her identity. "I am fond of my room, and have retreated here more and more of late years," she reports, "[h]ere are all my pictures" (69). The room is, of course, not only her cubicle in the Vancouver house, but her own psyche, wherein all her photographs of the past truly exist, like Morag's "Memorybank Movies." Hagar retreats to the comforting world of the photographs on two occasions when she feels most insecure, most afraid of being disinherited by being sent to the Silverthreads Nursing Home. It is, therefore, appropriate that she should seek refuge in contemplating the visual proof of her inheritance: her family photographs. This use of the ancestral photograph to validate one's identity is a common motif of modern and postmodern literature, particularly in works which concern themselves with the facts and fictions which the human psyche weaves around itself. Witness, for example, Lisa Erdman's triumphant presentation of this unassailable evidence to Dr. Sigmund Freud in D. M. Thomas's novel, *The White Hotel*:

> And one day she stormed in with an air of triumph. She flourished before me two photographs. One, somewhat brown and tattered, was of her mother's grave, and the other, a fresh photograph, was of her uncle's. . . . To my surprise, the dates of death on the two graves, faint but discernible, were the same. I had to admit that I was impressed, and that the balance of evidence such as it was, had swung towards her version of events. (124-25)

Hagar wishes not to prove a particular version of events in her communion with the photographs, but to validate her place in the Currie dynasty. It is interesting to note, for instance, that she concentrates on two different lines of ancestry on the two occasions that she consults her family photographs: the matriarchal and the patriarchal. Hagar's first attempt to discover a direct line of inheritance from her mother is frustrated; the daguerreotype of her young mother reveals to her only "a spindly and anxious girl, rather plain, ringleted stiffly." Hagar can find no connection between this meek countenance and her own "awful strength." Even physically, Hagar feels no sense of relatedness to this pathetic figure: "Dan and Matt inherited her daintiness while I was big-boned and husky as an ox" (59). This sense of unrelatedness, of otherness, is in turn validated for us when we see, through Hagar's eyes, the photograph of herself, taken when she was approximately the same age as her mother in the daguerreotype: "Not beautiful, I admit, not that china figurine look some women have, all gold and pink fragility. . . . Handsomeness lasts longer . . . " (60). In the final event, Hagar's own photograph asserts her identity more strongly than the photograph of her mother ever could; the inheritance from her maternal ancestor remains, like the meek visage peering out of the gilt frame, uncertain: "But still she peers perplexed out of her little frame . . . " (59).

The polar opposite of this quizzical glance is the robust glare of the photographed Jason Currie, which Hagar confronts on the second occasion that she studies her family photographs. "There's Father with his plumed moustache, coldly eyeing the camera, daring it not to do him justice." Here, in the patriarchal line of descent, Hagar finds the source of her own defiant outlook on the rest of the world. As though in visual representation of this legacy of defiance, Laurence has Hagar survey, on the same occasion, a childhood photograph of herself and of *her* male heirs, Marvin and John. The photographs themselves represent the effects of the Currie inflexibility on the heirs of the dynasty; Marvin looks uncomfortable in a sailor suit which speaks of Hagar's pretensions, his face characteristically "blank as water." John's pose, standing beside a wren in a white cage, speaks volumes as well about the emotional imprisonment which Hagar will force upon him.

Brampton Shipley, however, stands outside the patriarchal procession and also, significantly, outside Hagar's attempt to fix him photographically. "I have no picture of Brampton Shipley, my husband. I never asked for one, and he was not the type to have his picture taken unasked" (69). Besides suggesting that Hagar has not seen Bram clearly all along, this lack of a photograph also speaks of Bram's power, his refusal to be composed by Hagar. "Well listen here, Hagar, let's get one thing straight. I talk the way I talk, and I ain't likely to change now. If it's not good enough, that's too damn bad" (71). Hagar's late acceptance of Bram's energy and incorrigibility parallels the lesson learned by writer and photographer Eudora Welty, that the greatest element in her fictional photographs is "a single, entire human being, who will never be confined in any frame" (90).

To pursue this argument further, Susan Sontag argues that "[t]o take a picture is to have an interest in things as they are, in the *status quo* remaining unchanged (at least for as long as it takes to get a 'good' picture) . . ." (*On Photography* 12). Sontag's generalization does not apply satisfactorily to war or social protest photography (photographers who showed the effects of napalm bombs on Vietnamese babies were not, one hopes, supporting the *status quo*), but it does apply well to Hagar's relationship with Bram. That is, she could never capture a still shot of a man whom she fought constantly to *change*. Secondly, Sontag's belief that to photograph any object accords it value (*On Photography* 28) applies equally well to Hagar. Her refusal to ask for a photograph of Bram is an index of the low value which she placed on him during their marriage. Only now does it occur to her to wonder "if he would have liked me to ask for a picture of himself, even once?" (69).

Photography and possession, as we noted in relation to *Coming Through Slaughter*, are often synonymous. Often the possession of the portrait of a beloved one is a metaphor for the possession of the beloved. One thinks, for instance, of Jay Gatsby's collection of newspaper clippings about Daisy Buchanan in *The Great Gatsby*, or Arabella's possession – and later rejection – of Jude's photograph in Thomas Hardy's *Jude the Obscure*. Similarly, Hagar's sudden desire to have a photograph of Bram "as he was when we were first married" (69), is a desire to appropriate Bram, to recognize her true kinship to him. In fact, in the latter stages of her life Hagar *becomes* the likeness of Bram which was she never able to commit to paper, cursing, blurting her sharp-edged retorts, refusing to be "fixed" and "composed" herself. Moreover, the desire to appropriate Bram's image represents Hagar's suppressed desire to possess his body – note especially that she wants a photograph of Bram as he appeared during the first days of their marriage. Compare Elizabeth Barrett's opinion of photographic mementoes, voiced in a letter to Mary Russell Mitford in 1843:

I long to have such a memorial of every being dear to me in the world. It is not merely the likeness which is precious in such cases – but the association and the

sense of nearness involved in the thing ... the fact of
the *very shadow of the person* lying there fixed forever!
(qtd. in Sontag 183)

Although Bram is no Robert Browning, Hagar can share
Barrett's wonder at the visual immediacy of the photograph
largely because she has shifted her focus away from Bram's
verbal abilities. Her past comments about her unruly husband
concentrate frequently on his use (or, more properly, misuse) of
words: "He couldn't string two words together without some
crudity, that man" (79), she exclaims, and: *"This here! That there!
Don't you know anything?"* (71). Even Bram's sexual appetite
becomes comparable to bad verbal manners: "he would say he
was sorry, sorry to bother me, as though it were an affliction
with him, something that set him apart, as his speech did, from
educated people" (116). Words are even partially responsible
for Hagar's decision to marry Bram – the words of Lottie
Dreiser, that Bram is "Common as dirt . . . " (47). "How clearly
her words come to mind," Hagar now reflects, "[i]f she'd not
said them, would I have done as I did? Hard to say. How silly
the words seem now" (47–48). Such words do, indeed, seem
silly to Hagar now, especially when she realizes that Bram alone
was the wielder of a more tender, respectful word: "Hagar"
(80). Her admission, then, as she looks at her other photographs, that "[w]hatever anyone *said* of him, no one could deny
he was a good-*looking* man" (69; emphasis added), carries more
emotional weight and awareness than one might at first suspect. Hagar has found her "photograph" of Bram.

"The world is even smaller now" (282), thinks Hagar as her
life draws to a close, and there is a very real sense in *The Stone
Angel* of the progressive tunnelling of vision as one grows old.
For the inhabitants of Silverthreads Nursing Home, photographs are one example of the ever-narrowing confines of life.
"It's that Mrs. Steiner," one of the women warns Hagar during
her visit there, "[o]nce she gets going with those photographs,
you'll never hear the end of it" (102). For these people, cut off
from normal family relationships, the photograph becomes the
narrow remnant of that fuller life. Unfortunately, these photographs cannot even be communicated to others. All that Hagar
sees when Mrs. Steiner proudly displays the photograph of her
grandchildren is "[t]wo perfectly ordinary children . . . playing

145

on a teeter-totter" (103). Here, the photograph is not as much a living link with the past as a ragged remnant, which can, furthermore, only be decoded and appreciated by an audience of one.

This association between photography and an ever-narrowing world view finds its most extreme expression in the x-rays performed upon Hagar's body. As critics have mentioned, Hagar as an old woman feels trapped in her own body (Thomas, *Margaret Laurence* 36). Corresponding to that reductive sensation is the internal photograph, which ultimately reveals the growth which kills her. While she is being physically x-rayed, Hagar discovers corresponding emotional cancers in her past: her gruff treatment of Marvin, her snobbish disdain at "serving a bunch of breeds and ne'er-do-wells" at threshing time, and her progressive alienation from Bram (114). When Hagar tries to reach out to the past, using the internal voice which is reminiscent of Rachel Cameron ("*Bram, listen – ,*"), she is brusquely thrust back into the present moment, feeling "naked, exposed to the core of my head" (116). One can gaze at the objects depicted in photographs, but one can never reenter the world of the photograph and change it to one's liking.

In *The Stone Angel*, Laurence establishes the motif which resurfaces in *The Diviners* in a more self-conscious fashion: a woman gazing at her photographs. More importantly, she handles photographic vision in a sensitive, complex way, by revealing that it is curiously both expansive (in its invoking of memory) and reductive (in its fragmentary and unalterable nature). In fact, the last stages of Hagar Shipley's life resemble an old family portrait, with an oval black background. The images appeared in this shape because early cameras produced circular images on square negatives. To A.D. Coleman, these black borders suggest

> psychologically, a form of 'tunnel vision,' the gradual but inexorable shrinking of peripheral visual perception which accompanies old age and accelerates toward the end – that 'dying of the light' against which Dylan Thomas urged his father's rage. (165)

Given Laurence's epigraph to *The Stone Angel*: "Do not go gentle into that good night. / Rage, rage against the dying of the light," these meditations are hauntingly apt. If Hagar Shipley's journey into death does resemble the encroaching blackness of an old photograph, one can at least say that she has seized the opportunity to look back into the photographic images of the past and has made her peace with them, before the "dying of the light."

✤ A Jest of God (1966) ✤

Rachel Cameron, too, is a creature whose inner darkness threatens to overwhelm and choke her life; it is no coincidence that she should be likened at one point to "the negative of a photograph" (29). As Clara Thomas points out, Rachel, unlike Hagar, lives almost entirely in the present: "she can hardly ever see through to another Rachel, or to a wider world ... " (*Margaret Laurence* 53). It is, therefore, impossible in Rachel's stifling world of the present to conceive of the photograph as a liberating artifact, for that conception, as we have seen in the works of Findley and Ondaatje, is usually attended by a concern for the past, for history. Instead, the photograph, cut off from the contexts which could give it positive value, becomes an agent of fixity or ambiguity to Rachel.

Fixity is the ruling principle of Rachel Cameron's life. "I can't move, that's the awful thing. I'm hemmed in, caught" bemoans Rachel at the fateful Tabernacle meeting (30). In a compulsive reaction to the outpourings of the inner lives of the Tabernacle members, Rachel feels her own body, her speech-producing muscles especially, become paralyzed: "The muscles of my face have wired my jawbone so tightly" (34), and later she says: "I can feel my every muscle becoming rigid" (35). After the episode of speaking in tongues, and of Calla's lesbian advances, Rachel, like Hagar, turns to stone: "I hold myself very carefully when she's near, like a clay figurine, easily broken, unmendable" (46). Later, pondering her father's unfulfilled life while talking to Hector Jonas, Rachel realizes the psychological rigidity which she has imposed upon her own life: *"The life he wanted most. If my father had wanted otherwise, it would have been otherwise. Not necessarily better, but at least different. Did* he ever try to alter it? Did I, with mine?" (124–25). Rachel's altering of her life by moving to Vancouver, like her mournful cry in the Tabernacle and her sexual awakening with Nick, all represent moments when her customary fixity loosens, when the "clay figurine" begins to crack and come to life.

Rachel's vision similarly alternates between rigidity and emotional flux. Her tense waking moments, when she must deal with the trivial comments and questions of her mother, or of the members of the Bridge Club, give way to wild sexual fantasies during the interminable nights. As George Bowering notes, Rachel's fantasies must take place outside the confines of the town – either in a forest, or on a beach, or in an exotic Egyptian setting ("That Fool of a Fear" 212). When Rachel enacts those sexual desires with Nick, however, she craves the protection of a house with four walls and a roof. Furthermore, these nights, full of restless thought and dreams, are hardly a satisfying release for Rachel; even they are inescapable, hemming her in. At one point, she describes the night as an ever-turning Ferris wheel upon which she is glued "or wired, like paper, like a photograph, insubstantial, unable to anchor myself, unable to stop this slow nocturnal circling" (18). The image of the photograph on the ferris wheel captures powerfully in an almost *symboliste* manner the grinding tension between control and the unconscious in Rachel's mind.

This wild alternation of fixity and flux is also captured in the telescoped nature of Rachel's vision. Her perception of objects and events ranges wildly from the neurotically microscopic to the hazily impressionistic. As Rachel herself realizes,

> Something must be the matter with my way of viewing things. I have no middle view. Either I fix on a detail and see it as though it were magnified ... or else the world recedes and becomes blurred, artificial, indefinite, an abstract painting of a world. (85)

For example, while Rachel speaks to Willard Siddley, she cannot help focusing on the "skin on his hands ... speckled, sun-spotted" and the "small hairs" that "sprout even from his knuckles" (8). This microscopic vision tends to be associated with Rachel's sexual impulses; she realizes, with some shock, that she had wanted to touch Willard's hands, "[t]o see what the hairs felt like" (9), and she later muses over the minute details of Nick's body – his hair, muscles, and skin. When she learns of Nick's departure from Manawaka, however, Rachel returns to the detached vision which she exhibits at the beginning of the novel (looking at the children from a window, seeming to watch herself breaking a ruler over James Doherty's nose). "People were sitting there, waiting, suitcases at their feet," she numbly reflects, "but they had no faces.... [T]heir faces were unfocused and hidden to me ..." (152). Whereas Hagar Shipley's visual development might be compared to bringing sensual, concrete detail gradually into focus, as a camera or telescope does, Rachel's is more akin to viewing experience through the opposite ends of a telescope, one after the other, in confusing succession.

This nervous flight from claustrophobic detail to hazy ambiguity is reflected also in Rachel's response to visual art. As George Bowering has noted, Laurence "presents to the reader sitting behind Rachel's eyes a number of ikons," but for reasons which go beyond the revelation of the town's "kitschy insularity," in Bowering's words ("That Fool" 212). The icons which reveal Rachel's visual schizophrenia include, for example, the diametrically opposed representations of Christ in Calla's Tabernacle and in the more conservative church attended by Rachel's mother. The paintings of Jesus which hang in the Tabernacle show him "bearded and bleeding, his heart exposed and bristling with thorns like a scarlet pincushion" (30). Again, painfully detailed vision is associated with strong emotion – in this case religious – and the image of the exposed heart reflects Rachel's own morbid fear of exposing her emotions. The picture of Jesus which hangs in the more sedate town church is, by comparison, abstract and emotionally detached, showing "a pretty and clean-cut Jesus expiring gently and with absolutely no inconvenience, no gore, no pain, just this nice and slightly effeminate insurance salesman who, somewhat incongruously, happens to be clad in a toga ..." (41). Like Holman Hunt's painting of the knight and lady in The Stone Angel, this icon represents a loftily detached, abstract passion, albeit religious. In addition, the juxtaposition of Rachel's visits to the two churches in chapters 2 and 3 emphasizes the frenetic, constant shifting of Rachel's telescope vision – from dangerous realism to stifling idealism.

149

Two corresponding icons which we see through Rachel's eyes add complexity to the battle between realism and detachment which is raging within her. Rachel praises the intricate drawing of a spaceship done by James Doherty, the child for whom Rachel feels such warmth that she feels compelled to distance herself from him in telescopic fashion. The drawing appeals to Rachel largely because of its "many detailed parts," yet these details are, significantly, fantastic and imaginative ("hydroponic containers for growing vegetables in mid-space, weird protuberances which have some absolute necessity ... " [5]). This reconciliation of detail and idealism (body and spirit) is precisely what Rachel is searching for; and Nick Kazlik, because of his own emotional detachment, can only supply the former. Nevertheless, Rachel symbolically rejects this compromise; she bestows the same word of praise upon the next child's drawing, "a lady of appalling unoriginality," copied from a colouring book (6). Rachel has again fled from passionate, imaginative realism to safe and detached mediocrity and she will continue to do so. She reverses this act only when she leaves Manawaka and embraces a portrait of herself which, like James's drawing, mingles realism and romance: "I may become, in time, slightly more eccentric.... I will be lonely, almost certainly.... I will rage in my insomnia like a prophetess" (201–02).

In addition to fixing or distancing external reality, Rachel's camera eye may also transform it into her own private, fictional film. In particular, Rachel becomes addicted to replaying more comforting versions of her relationship with Nick in her mind: " – Darling – I left in a hell of a hurry" (154), and: "Listen, darling, do you think life as a Grade Eleven teacher's wife would be a fate worse than – " (116). At one point, Rachel reconstructs an entire scene to her liking (129–30), and while she is sitting in the Parthenon Café, mourning Nick's absence, she creates a scene which could catch the reader off guard: " – Rachel. She looks up, startled, and he is standing there. Standing here, right here in the Parthenon Café" (165–66). Only the dash preceding the paragraph (a device which resurfaces in *The Fire-Dwellers*) and the insistent, unbelieving repetition of the word "here" warn the vigilant reader that this is a fantasy and not a melodramatic twist of plot. Laurence's implication and tricking of the reader in this instance resembles the deceptive replaying of scenes in extremely self-conscious novels such as Hubert Aquin's *Blackout*. Ambiguity, to borrow a phrase from *The Diviners*, is everywhere (309).

The ultimate ambiguity – and the ultimate clash between realism and fiction – is contained in the photograph of Nick Kazlik which Rachel "misreads." ("Misreads" is perhaps a misleading term, since the misunderstanding involves a crossing up of verbal and visual messages between Nick and Rachel; John Moss's wry comment that "[v]erbal confusion leads to the end of the relationship" is only half right [*A Reader's Guide* 159].) Critics of the novel tend to assume that this photograph of "a boy whose face and eyes speak entirely of Nick" (149), is, in fact, of Nick, although Rachel wrongly assumes that it depicts his son (Stouck 249; Thomas, *Margaret Laurence* 51). Laurence's addition of the word "entirely" to a typescript version of the novel appears to support this idea (*A Jest of God* ts.). Nevertheless, Nick produces the photograph as a defense against Rachel's charge that he never says what he means. "I've said more than enough, about everything" (149), he claims, doubtless referring to the story of the death of his twin brother Steven, which he has uncharacteristically confided to Rachel. The photograph which he would be most likely to produce, therefore, at this moment, would be that of his brother. Since Nick cannot put into words the immense burden of guilt which he feels, he produces evidence of the tormenting visual image which he carries around within him: "Yours?" she asks. "Yes" he says, taking the picture away from her. "Mine" (149).

The perplexing ambiguities of this scene are built upon the ambiguity of the photographic image itself. "All photographs are ambiguous," claims John Berger – that is, until they are mediated by words (Berger and Mohr 91). Without words, however (or, with only Nick's inadequate or ambiguous words), the photograph is open to wild misinterpretation. Roland Barthes claims that a photograph sends two messages: "a denoted message, which is the *analogon* itself" ("a small boy") and "a connotated message" (17) (in Rachel's case, "Nick's son"), and it is the confusion of these two messages which produces the misunderstanding in *A Jest of God*. The distance between Nick's words and the meaning which Rachel ascribes to them has already been poignantly caught in the question which prompted Nick to produce the photograph in the first place: "Nick, why don't you ever *say* what you *mean*?" (149; emphasis added). This photograph in *A Jest of God* becomes a veritable emblem of the overwhelming difficulties involved in saying what one means, an emblem of the tremendous gap between words, images, and meaning.

+ *The Fire-Dwellers* (1969) +

Margaret Laurence's third Manawaka novel is the first of her writings which could be called "photofiction." Building on her evocative use of the photograph as a paradigm of human communication in *A Jest of God*, Laurence allows photography to become the major structuring device of *The Fire-Dwellers* – the means by which Stacey McAindra's story is communicated to us as readers. As Marcienne Rocard notes, "*C'est avec "Fire-Dwellers" ... que se produit la veritable cassure*" ("It is with *The Fire-Dwellers* that the real break [with Laurence's earlier fiction] comes" [113]).

For Laurence, this stylistic *cassure* was both a conscious aim and a hard-fought battle. On a sheet of paper which accompanies one of the typescripts of the novel, she sets out deliberately in a list the special typographical effects which she wants reflected in the final copy (*Fire-Dwellers* ts.). As she later explained, while writing *The Fire-Dwellers* she kept thinking: "What I want to get is the effect of voices and pictures – just voices and pictures ... It was only much later that I realized that 'voices and pictures' is only another – and to my mind, better – way of saying 'audio-visual' " ("Gadgetry or Growing" 88). Trying to capture Stacey McAindra's minute sensations, both conscious and unconscious, proved to be a heavy undertaking for Laurence; she burned one manuscript and, from the evidence of one typescript, evidently had much trouble with the highly visual "Ever-Open Eye" segments (*Fire-Dwellers* ts.).

Nevertheless, Laurence succeeded in her aim to write an audio-visual novel; Clara Thomas claims that this "technically ... most complex" of Laurence's works reveals "a fast-shuttering, multiscreen camera and soundtrack technique" (*Manawaka World* 124). The visual appearance of the writing, though not as photographically terse as that of Findley or Ondaatje, is closer to that of *The Wars* or *Coming Through Slaughter* than anything

Laurence had written. Marcienne Rocard notices that there is far less analysis in this novel (118) – one reason for the brevity of Laurence's paragraphs. Laurence's later comments on the style support this observation:

> I wanted the pictures – that is, the descriptions – whether in outer life or dreams or memories, to be as sharp and instantaneous as possible, and always brief, because it seemed to me that this is the way – or at least one way – life is perceived, in short sharp visual images which leap away from us even as we look at them. ("Gadgetry or Growing" 80)

One is reminded of Findley's comparison of the technique of *The Wars* to a billboard flashing photographs, or Alice Munro's belief that "[t]here are just flashes of things we know and find out" (Hancock 102).

Stacey does experience these flashes of insight – and despair – in an extremely cinematic fashion in *The Fire-Dwellers*. The "Ever-Open Eye" of the media camera constantly assaults Stacey, sometimes in the midst of her most private thoughts: "In God's name, what is *Mac* like, in there, wherever he lives? EVER-OPEN EYE   THE SON OF ROBIN HOOD IS CANTERING ALONG THROUGH SHERWOOD" (126). At other times, this intrusive eye mirrors the chaos of Stacey's domestic microcosm:

> THIS IS THE EIGHT-O'CLOCK NEWS BOMBING RAIDS
> LAST NIGHT DESTROYED FOUR VILLAGES IN
> Mum! Where's my social studies scribbler? (91)

In both cases, the "Eye" represents a terrifying macrocosm which drives Stacey even further into her own private world.

Even in her inner world, however, Stacey cannot avoid the "Ever-Open Eye" any more than she can avoid the horrors of the contemporary world; both are present in microcosmic form in her own psyche. Stacey is, in fact, an ever-open photographic eye – and an extremely sensitive one at that. The novel opens with her gazing at the images reflected in her bedroom mirror, "distanced by the glass like humans on TV, less real than real and yet more sharply focused because isolated and limited by a frame" (3). The events of Stacey's private life (the images in the bedroom mirror) may, indeed, appear to be distanced from contemporary world affairs, and yet, Laurence suggests in this densely suggestive passage, they focus even more clearly the global chaos. The "limited," framed nature of these photographic images does not diminish, but increases and concentrates their power, just as a photograph implicitly suggests, through its isolation of worldly detail, the overwhelming complexity of the world beyond the photograph. Thus, photography, in this important context, contains a justification for the narrative method which Margaret Laurence has chosen for *The Fire-Dwellers*: the sudden juxtaposition of microcosm and macrocosm, private and public life.

Stacey's photographic eye has, in fact, been implicitly related to this scheme of juxtaposing the large and the small in the novel. Clara Thomas has perceptively commented that "[t]he consciousness of Stacey Cameron is like an eye: its pupil expands to accept her world, then contracts in terror; the movement is a halting, opening and shutting, a broadening and then a narrowing ..." (*Manawaka World* 122). One perfect illustration of this eye movement is Stacey's refusal to look at the child who has been hit by a car; only weeks later does the news that the boy was a friend of Ian's filter down into her consciousness; significantly, through a private source – Ian himself. The camera is built on the same model as the eye, however, with the lens and shutter performing the same action as the human pupil, and Laurence uses both models to describe Stacey at Buckle's apartment: "None of this [the furnishings] creates more than a momentary flicker on Stacey's eye camera" (157). The camera, as a model, therefore, serves two of Laurence's purposes in *The Fire-Dwellers*: it allows her to fulfil her Joycean aim of "trying to get across the vast number of things which impinge upon the individual consciousness every minute of the day," as she once expressed it ("Gadgetry or Growing" 86), and it reveals the bitter conflict between subjective and objective reality being waged inside Stacey's psyche.

In *The Fire-Dwellers*, the subjective counterpart to the "Ever-Open Eye" is what Laurence calls in *The Diviners* the "innerfilm" – Stacey's most private vision. The most striking "innerfilm" in *The Fire-Dwellers* is Stacey's dream of being in a forest carrying an object which she discovers, to her horror, to be her own severed and bloody head. This nightmare vision raises the question of inner and outer sight; as Stacey in her dream asks: "*How is it that she can see it? What is she seeing it with? That is the question*" (124). This striking image of a woman gazing at her own bleeding head could serve as an emblem of *The Fire-Dwellers* and its visual method: How *does* one perceive one's own torments? Can one see such torments as objective, as detached from oneself, or will such an attempt only result in a psychological schism, a severed head?

The most terrifying images of the violence and alienation which occur outside the theatre of Stacey's mind are not the "Ever-Open Eye" sequences, but the photographs from newspapers. Here, too, Laurence's aim is to frame and isolate an image to increase its impact on the viewer:

> There was this newspaper picture of this boy some city in the States kid about twelve Negro kid you know shot by accident it said by the police in a riot and he was just lying there ... and his eyes were wide open and you wondered what he was seeing. (193)

This description is based on a photograph which Laurence actually saw of a child accidentally shot by the police in a Detroit riot. "He was lying on the sidewalk, and his eyes were open," Laurence recalls, "[h]e was seeing everything, I guess, including himself." In both accounts, the image of seeing one's own bleeding body occurs, as in Stacey's nightmare vision. Even the distancing camera-eye proffers no comfort, either to Laurence or to Stacey. Laurence claims that after putting the photograph away, the face of the child "kept fluctuating in my mind. Sometimes it was the face of your son," she imagines herself saying to his mother, "sometimes of mine" (*Heart of a Stranger* 202). Similarly, Stacey reflects on the "Ever-Open Eye" photographs of horror: "I see it and then I don't see it. It becomes pictures. And you wonder about the day when you open your door and find they've been filming those pictures in your street" (305). For Stacey and for Laurence, the battle between subjectivity and objectivity rages on, like an unquenchable fire. To use the anatomical model, as long as the eye perceives, it must both admit and reject light.

The final photographic symbols of this ongoing battle are the wedding picture of Stacey and Mac and the photographs of their children. The description of these photographs appears twice, near the beginning and the end of *The Fire-Dwellers*, lending them a significance not unlike the photograph of Doris and Mervyn Ondaatje in *Running in the Family*. The wedding picture, described at the end of the book, speaks of youthful hope and ambition: "Stacey twenty-three, almost beautiful although not knowing it then, and Mac twenty-seven, hopeful confident lean" (305). The introductory description, however, includes a bitterly sarcastic gloss by Stacey: "Agamemnon King of men or the equivalent, at least to her" (4). The omission of this aside in the later description suggests that Stacey's bitterness has been exorcised, that if she no longer expects Mac to be Agamemnon, perhaps she can now cease to feel herself a guilty Clytemnestra.

In terms of the battle between the perceiver and the object, the photograph's reappearance suggests that the images of Stacey's marriage and children are still there, still to be perceived, reevaluated, and, occasionally, to be not entirely believed in. Joan Hind-Smith's interpretation of the photograph, that "[l]ife is the same, but not quite, because Stacey has accepted her lot" thus appears too complacent (45), especially given the fact that Mac and Stacey engage in fresh domestic warfare immediately after the last description of the wedding photograph. It would doubtless be more cheering to see the repetition of the marital photograph as a reaffirmation, a closed circle like a wedding ring, yet one of Stacey's final queries: "Will the fires go on, inside and out?" (307), reminds us that the battle between the eye and the world never ends – that the only circle to be drawn in Stacey's world is a circle of fire.

✦ *A Bird in the House* (1970) ✦

Margaret Laurence's shift in perspective – from the generation of Rachel and Stacey to the earlier generations of her own parents and grandparents – has a startling effect on her use of photography as a metaphor. *A Bird in the House* is Laurence's *Running in the Family*, and the family photograph album becomes the dominant photographic image, as in Ondaatje's fictionalized memoir. In Laurence's work, however, the family portrait is dimmer – seldom the emblem of fervent belief in generation and familial affection that it is in Ondaatje; more often, a ghostly reminder of a death-filled past.

In particular, this sombre mood is associated with the photographs of Vanessa MacLeod's (and Laurence's) parents and grandparents. When Vanessa's mother is near death at the birth of her second child, Vanessa wanders gloomily among the "outmoded clothing and old photograph albums" in the unused rooms of the house (42). The photographs which captivate her are the "silver framed photographs of Uncle Roderick – as a child, as a boy, as a man in his Army uniform" (43). We are, of course, back in the world of Robert Ross in *The Wars* and John Harris in *The Last of the Crazy People* – youthful figures whose photographic images underscore the bizarre clash between youth and death. It is, therefore, appropriate that Vanessa should contemplate such icons at a time when birth and death seem about to collide in her own life. Significant, too, is the fact that the threat of the mother's disappearance continues to revive thoughts of death in Vanessa – thoughts which are associated, like those of Hooker Winslow in *The Last of the Crazy People*, with the photographed ancestors. When her mother leaves to care for Grandmother Connor in "The Mask of the Bear," Vanessa mourns that "[w]ithout my mother, our house seemed like a museum, full of dead and meaningless objects, vase, and and gilt-framed pictures ..." (79). Without the mother – the symbol of life and generation – the child feels the full force of mortality oppressing her.

As Vanessa grows older, this aura of death surrounding the photographs – and lives – of her forbears grows ever stronger. A few years later, the vision of the "stretches of mud" (94), which Vanessa has seen in her father Ewen's photographs of the war, gains new horror for her, for she now realizes the burden of guilt which he carries with him for his brother Roderick's death. Photographs become weapons in this family battle of guilt and responsibility: Ewen's mother, Vanessa notes, surrounds her bed with "half a dozen framed photos of Uncle Roderick and only one of my father ..." (107). Only after Ewen dies unexpectedly does remorse set in for Grandmother MacLeod – remorse which, like that of Hagar, involves the possession of photographs and the valuation of a loved one: "I left her in the bedroom ... looking at the picture of my father that had been taken when he graduated from medical college.

Maybe she was sorry now that she had only the one photograph of him, but whatever she felt, she did not say" (109).

The most moving emblem of this battle between vitality and death is Vanessa's ritual burning of the photograph of a European girl with a "sweetly sad posed smile" which she finds in Ewen MacLeod's desk after his death (112). This photograph, a relic of his adventures overseas as a young man, embodies all of the emotional freedom and vitality which the MacLeod household (to say nothing of the Connor household) would frown upon. As she burns the photograph, Vanessa realizes that her father, living in a harsh Puritan environment, had to keep a great portion of his emotional life locked inside himself, like the photograph locked up in his desk: "As I watched the smile of the girl turn into scorched paper, I grieved for my father as though he had just died now" (113).

Vanessa's burning of the photograph is a symbolic rejection of the enclosed life her parents and grandparents lived. Indeed, the photographs associated with Vanessa's generation in *A Bird in the House* speak of wider ambitions and dreams, and of life rather than death. Family connections and reputation mean far less to Vanessa than to Grandfather Connor or Grandmother MacLeod, and so too do their emblems, the family photographs. She banishes all thought of her cousin Chris's needy relatives: "His sisters did not exist for me," she claims, "not even as photographs, because I did not want them to exist. I wanted him to belong only here" (134). Vanessa wants to rewrite the story of Chris's past, as he too wants to do, to allow him to begin life fresh – just as Morag Gunn will desire to rewrite her past in *The Diviners*. Chris's ambitions only have reality in his mind – and, symbolically, in photographs: "You ever seen a really big bridge, Vanessa? Well, I haven't either, but I've seen pictures" (135-36). Futile these dreams, or attempts to block out the past may be, yet they represent a step forward from Ewen MacLeod's generation, when dreams and inner lives had to be carefully locked away in a desk drawer.

The vibrance of Vanessa's photographs also stands in opposition to the death-filled images of the ancestral photograph albums. As a child, she devours the "picture-filled pages" of *National Geographic* magazine, "as though I were on the verge of some discovery" (54). The exotic images of orchids and leopards which she discovers there are diametrically opposed to the order which Grandmother MacLeod imposes on the family while Vanessa's mother is ill. Grandmother MacLeod scolds Vanessa for scattering the magazines about, and at the end of the story, Vanessa senses the conflict between her love of heterogeneity, of exoticism, and Grandmother MacLeod's demand for order. Pondering the "accidents" of life, such as the still birth of her sister, Vanessa thinks immediately of the "pictures of leopards and green seas" and senses "their strangeness, their disarray." Vanessa's final conclusion confirms that she has chosen a vital and diverse world (one which nevertheless includes suffering and death) instead of an ordered world; lush, dangerous photographs instead of the starched and deathly photographs of the ancestral albums: "I felt that whatever God might love in this world, it was certainly not order" (59).

+ *The Diviners* (1974) +

It is left to Morag Gunn to discover what Vanessa MacLeod resists so strongly: that life, memory, and fiction may reconcile order and randomness. The symbols of this "ordered absence," to use Margaret Atwood's term, are the photographs of Morag's past which she carefully arranges in chronological order at the beginning of *The Diviners*. These six photographs are fictional analogues; Morag's arrangement and embroidering of them represents in miniature Laurence's composition of *The Diviners* – a novel composed of six sections, if one includes, as one should, the "Album" section at the end of the novel.

These photographs, placed at the beginning of Morag's (and Laurence's) chronicle, tend to be viewed by critics as a separate stylistic technique, a type of opening gimmick (Woodcock 205). Leona Gom claims that "the use of photographs ... is not a sustained technique, and may at best represent frozen frames in Morag's longer mental movies" (51). Michel Fabre sees such devices as separable from the intense self-consciousness of the novel: "More interesting than Margaret Laurence's attempt at 'audio-visual fiction' in *The Diviners* is her repeated affirmation that reading and writing are not only complementary but also homothetic or homologous activities" (278). When one looks closer, however, one finds that Morag's photographs are not merely dangling fragments of her "Memorybank Movies"; they are separate visual icons which work in tandem with the movies. Moreover, they work in tandem to comment on the very acts of reading and writing.

The six photographs which take us from Morag as an embryo ("a little fish, connected unthinkingly with life" [6]) to a child of five years represent the genesis of the artist and of fiction itself. Morag is enclosed in all of the photographs save the last: in her mother's womb, in the yard, behind a gate, leaning out a window, and in a room. In the last photograph, Morag is surrounded by dark spruce trees, yet she builds a tent-like dwelling of her own out of couchgrass, where she sings songs and invents playmates called "Rosa Picardy" and "Cowboy Joke," names born of the song-legends. This making and inventing is, of course, the genesis of Morag's profession as a writer. Also, by the time we read the description of this couchgrass haven, after reading the five preceding fictionalized versions of Morag's photographs, we fully expect this memory to be an invented one as well. Fiction and imagination, however, have become more real to Morag than genealogical fact: "*I remember those imaginary characters better than I do my parents,*" she confesses (11).

The conflict between order and disorder which we noted in *A Bird in the House* is also present in Morag's photographs, and is directly related to the idea of fictionalizing the past. The mind, of course, thinks and recalls in a random, non-chronological fashion, yet Laurence defends her use of the photographic sequence by explaining in an interview with Michel Fabre that "Morag is a writer and she is deliberately setting out to construct her life and of course the novel she is writing is *The Diviners*" (205). (One is reminded of the character of Bernard in André Gide's *The Counterfeiters*, who is in the process of writing a novel entitled *The Counterfeiters*.) On the level of the photographic image itself, one often witnesses the interplay of order and disorder. The photographer Berenice Abbott once said that the photographer's challenge is "to impose order onto the things seen and to supply the visual context and the intellectual framework" (Burgin 111). Yet by imposing order, the photographer changes the object – or, at least, the manner in which it is perceived. Umberto Eco thus argues that "the theory of the photograph as an analogue to reality" has been abandoned; that the photograph is analogous to our retinal image alone (Eco 33). The application of this debate to Morag's fictionalized recreation of her past (and to Ondaatje's *Running in the Family*) is clear: perception and memory become inseparable from an objective past, and fiction becomes inseparable – as in Agee and Evans's *Let Us Now Praise Famous Men* – from documentary. Morag's double response to her photographs, therefore, represents more than an example of her gruff, undercutting manner; it represents this entire conflict between fiction and fact, order and chaos:

> *I've kept them, of course, because something in me doesn't want to lose them, or perhaps doesn't dare. Perhaps they're my totems, or contain a portion of my spirit. Yeh, and perhaps they are exactly what they seem to be – a jumbled mess of old snapshots. . . . (5)*

"Memorybank Movies" take over from the still photographs early in the novel, yet the two visual forms work together to reproduce the processes of memory and narration. Victor Burgin has written that a photograph is a fragment which implies "a world of causes, of 'before and after,' of 'if, then . . . ,' a *narrated* world" (211). One could describe Morag's mental shift from her fictionalized photographs to the "Memorybank Movies" as a search for "a world of causes"; after recalling the imaginary playmates whom she created when her mother and father were ill, she recognizes that her "memories" involve "only what was happening to Me. What was happening to everyone else? What really happened in the upstairs bedroom?" (11). These are not only a grown woman's questions about her past; they are the novelist's questions as well, the impulse to ask "and then?" of which E. M. Forster writes in *Aspects of the Novel*. Furthermore, Victor Burgin writes of this larger context of the photograph in cinematic terms: "the significance of the photograph goes beyond its literal signification by way of the routes of primary processes . . . the individual photograph becomes the point of origin of a series of psychic 'pans' and 'dissolves' " (211). The point of origin, the photograph, represents in *The Diviners* the human point of origin, childhood; when Pique enters Morag's world, the "Memorybank Movie" pattern is temporarily disrupted, and we see once again a succession of childhood photographs.

As Morag implies, the movement from photograph to "Memorybank Movie" involves a shift away from the exclusive self to the self interacting with others. Morag, therefore, like Rachel and Stacey, becomes a camera; as Clara Thomas remarks: "Morag comes to us then as perforce a watcher" (*Manawaka World* 135), although she makes no distinction between Morag watching photographs and Morag watching the "Memorybank Movies." The "Memorybank Movies," however, reveal Morag not as a spectator of the past, but as a spectator *in* the past. For example, early in the novel, Morag constructs a mental "still-shot" of Christie Logan's house, in the type of exacting detail which would earn Del Jordan's praise in *Lives of Girls and Women*. Morag catches herself up, as in the passages dealing with her photographs, realizing that *"I didn't see it in that detail at first. I guess I must have seen it as a blur. How did it feel?"* To answer her own question, Morag must attempt to place herself in the world of the past; the first word of the "Memorybank Movie" which follows is her answer – "Smelly" (24).

For all of these attempts on Morag's part to find answers to questions like "how?" and "what really happened?", the "Memorybank Movies" are just as fictionalized as the photographs. "She could not even be sure of their veracity," we read at one point, "nor guess how many times they had been refilmed," like Rachel's films in *A Jest of God* (23). Dialogues, too, such as the comic-grotesque discussion of Morag's pregnancy with her landlady, Maggie Teffler ("You preggers, kid?" [241]), convey an air of veracity, yet Morag holds dialogues with Catharine Parr Traill in this fashion as well. Therefore, the "Memorybank Movies," although they dramatize the process of searching for cause and effect in the past, are themselves fictions – not unassailable fact. Rather, one feels, the process itself is of worth in *The Diviners*, just as Morag travels to Scotland to discover her ancestry and discovers nothing there except the fact that Canada and not Scotland is her home. "The myths are my reality," she concludes (319), and one feels that the same is ultimately true of her fictionalized films and photographs.

A second type of cinematic device which Laurence uses is the "Innerfilm," which has been treated by critics of the novel as a type of subsection of the "Memorybank Movie." Actually, the "Innerfilms" are qualitatively different, for they depict events which have no referents outside Morag's mind (unlike her "Memorybank Movies" of her life with Christie and Prin, which have, if not absolute veracity, some basis in fact). Rather, the "Innerfilm" is pure ego idealization, perceptions of the ideal past or future. Thus, in her "Innerfilm," the McConnell's Landing house becomes a comforting haven for Morag, the competent pioneer (338), whereas in the "Memorybank Movie," the cracking linoleum, aged furnace, and cold water ironically reproduce actual pioneering conditions. Two other "Innerfilms" reproduce Morag's youthful fantasies; seeing herself in melodramatic terms either as a wealthy authoress or as a corpse (who manages nevertheless to produce a masterpiece of posthumous fiction [101]). Again, Morag's life at McConnell's Landing, answering calls from readers who assume that she is wealthy, provides a sobering contrast (20).

Although they are not labelled "Innerfilms," the private colloquies which Morag holds with the spirit of Catharine Parr Traill do provide her with a certain amount of ego support. At first, Morag feels awed by her pioneering forbear, and pictures her as an inhabitant of the type of homestead which she pictured McConnell's Landing to be in her "Innerfilm":

> C.P.T. out of bed, fully awake, bare feet on the sliver-hazardous floorboards – no, take that one again. Feet on the homemade hooked rug.... Out to feed the chickens, stopping briefly on the way back to pull fourteen armloads of weeds.... (79)

Morag's "rewinding" of this "Innerfilm" allows her to cover up the hardships of pioneering life with the idealized portrait of the ever-resourceful pioneer (to cover up the metaphorical rough boards with a home-made rug of her own devising, so to speak). Nevertheless, by the time that "Saint C." pays her last visit, Morag feels enough confidence in her ability to cope in her personal wilderness that she declares: "I'm about to quit worrying about not being either an old or a new pioneer. So farewell, sweet saint ... " (332). Although Morag might not admit it, she has become a successful pioneer, and her inner dialogues with Catharine Parr Traill, unlike her fantastic "Innerfilms," show her working through the process of becoming a survivor in a modern wilderness. For this reason, all of Morag's films cease in part 5, "The Diviners," for her process of growth – like the process of writing *The Diviners* – has ended for the moment, and all that remains for Morag to do is "to write the remaining private and fictional words, and to set down her title" (370).

These words are not, however, the last to appear in the novel, and the presence of the songs and lyrics in the "Album" emphasizes the fact that written words and cameras are not the means by which all of the characters in *The Diviners* express themselves. Jules, like Bram, is an unphotographed – and unphotographable – man. Although he prizes a photograph of Pique as a baby, he refuses to have his own image recorded. "Maybe I'm superstitious," he explains, "[o]r maybe it's the same as I can't make up songs about myself. Maybe I don't want to see what I look like" (281). Once again, Laurence invokes the old fear of having one's identity stolen by the camera. In Jules's case, however, even the songs, which are his means of expression, must stop short of self-expression, probably because the Métis people, Laurence senses, feel bereft of any cultural identity to express.

This interpretation seems all the more likely when one considers that photographs (as well as words) have been the means by which the white settlers in Canada have preserved their identities. Christie Logan, for instance, directs his rage against those Manawaka citizens "who will be chucking out the family albums the moment the grandmother goes to her ancestors" (32–33). Christie salvages these unwanted cultural fragments and in doing so becomes a type of photographer or image collector himself. ("The photographer – and the consumer of photographs," Susan Sontag points out, "follow in the footsteps of the ragpicker, who was one of Baudelaire's favorite figures for the modern poet" [78].) Ironically, the photograph album which Christie drags home speaks eloquently of his own fallen place in the new world; the red velvet cover (symbolic of royalty or heraldry) is mouldy and has "no *family* name" (34). Similarly, Morag feels robbed of a heritage when she gazes at a group photograph of the 60th Canadian Field Artillery and cannot find her father's face. She thinks to herself: "it could be any one of them," but "[S]he says nothing" (72). Christie, however, does say something; he compensates for the lack of visual evidence by providing a legend – the sort of legend which Morag later treasures more than the most detailed of genealogical data. Although Morag can understand Jules's feeling of cultural loss to a certain extent, she is still not a complete cultural outcast; she finds herself in a more privileged cultural group which has the resources (and often the galling arrogance) to preserve its past through words, heraldic symbols, and, not least of all, photographs.

The Diviners has been christened by Anthony Appenzel "a kind of fictional compendium of Laurence's preoccupations as a writer . . . " (280). In the context of this study, the novel appears to be a compendium of the functions of photography in contemporary Canadian literature; the photograph as an analogue to memory and the fictional process, as a reminder of the past, as a haunting image of death or loss of identity, sometimes as an image of cultural continuity and belief in the fragile but enduring human chain. Morag Gunn can indeed speak for Canadian writers as seemingly diverse as Alice Munro, Timothy Findley, Michael Ondaatje, and Margaret Laurence herself, when she declares, *"I keep the snapshots not for what they show but for what is hidden in them"* (60).

WORKS CITED

Agee, James and Walker Evans. *Let Us Now Praise Famous Men: Three Tenant Families*. 1941. Boston: Houghton, 1960.

Aitken, Johan. " 'Long Live the Dead': An Interview with Timothy Findley." *Journal of Canadian Fiction* 33 (1982): 79-93.

Alter, Robert. *Partial Magic: The Novel as a Self-Conscious Genre*. Berkeley: U of California P, 1975.

Anderson, Sherwood. *Winesburg, Ohio: A Group of Tales of Ohio Small-Town Life*. New York: Huebach, 1919.

Austen, Jane. *Persuasion*. 1818. Ed. D.W. Harding. Harmondsworth, Eng: Penguin, 1978.

Barth, John. *Lost in the Funhouse: Fiction for Print, Tape, Live Voice*. New York: Bantam, 1968.

Barthes, Roland. *Image Music Text*. Trans. Stephen Heath. New York: Hill and Wang, 1977.

Benson, Eugene. " 'Whispers of Chaos': *Famous Last Words*." *World Literature Written in English* 21. 3 (1982): 599-606.

Berger, John and Jean Mohr. *Another Way of Telling*. New York: Pantheon, 1982.

Blott, Ann. " 'Stories to Finish': *The Collected Works of Billy the Kid*." *Studies in Canadian Literature* 2.2 (1977): 188-202.

Bowering, George. "Modernism Could Not Last Forever." *CanadianFiction Magazine* 32/33 (1979/80): 4-9.

_____. "That Fool of a Fear: Notes on *A Jest of God*." Woodcock 210-26.

Browning, Robert. "Fra Lippo Lippi." *Victorian Poetry*. Eds. E.K. Brown and J.O. Barley. New York: Ronald, 1962. 203-10.

Burgin, Victor. "Looking at Photographs." *Thinking Photography*. Ed. Victor Burgin. London: Macmillan, 1982. 142-53.

Cameron, Donald. *Conversations with Canadian Novelists: Part One*. Toronto: Macmillan, 1973.

Coldwell, Joan. "Alice Munro." *Oxford Companion to Canadian Literature*. Ed. William Toye. Toronto: Oxford UP, 1983.

_____. "Timothy Findley." *Oxford Companion to Canadian Literature*. Ed. William Toye. Toronto: Oxford UP, 1983.

Coleman, A.D. *Light Readings: A Photography Critic's Writings, 1968-1978*. New York: Oxford UP, 1979.

Conron, Brandon. "Munro's Wonderland." *Canadian Literature* 78 (1978): 109-10.

Dawson, Antony B. "Coming of Age in Canada." *Mosaic* 11.3 (1978): 47-62.

DeWiel, Alexa. "Mothers, Moons and Mafiosi." *Broadside* May 1983: 11-13.

Doyle, Sir Arthur Conan. *Essays on Photography*. Introd. John M. Gibson and Richard L. Green. London: Secker, 1982.

_____. "A Scandal in Bohemia." *The Adventures of Sherlock Holmes*. 1892. London: Pan, 1982. 15-40.

Eco, Umberto. "Critique of an Image." *Thinking Photography*. Ed. Victor Burgin. London: Macmillan, 1982. 32-38.

Eliot, T.S. *Collected Poems of T.S. Eliot, 1909-1962*. New York: Harcourt, 1963.

Fabre, Michel. "From *The Stone Angel* to *The Diviners*: An Interview with Margaret Laurence." Woodcock 276-87.

Findley, Timothy. "Alice Drops Her Cigarette on the Floor." *Canadian Literature* 91 (1981): 10-21.

_____. *The Butterfly Plague*. 1969. Rev. ed. Markham, ON: Penguin, 1986.

_____. *Can You See Me Yet?* Vancouver: Talon, 1977.

_____. "The Countries of Invention." *Canadian Literature* 100 (1984): 104-08.

_____. *Dinner Along the Amazon*. Markham, ON: Penguin, 1984.

_____. *Famous Last Words*. Toronto: Clarke, Irwin, 1981.

_____. *The Last of the Crazy People*. London: Macdonald, 1967.

_____. *Not Wanted on the Voyage*. Toronto: Viking-Penguin, 1984.

_____. "The Novel as Film/The Film as Novel." Lecture. Conference on "Canadian Fiction and the Art of Film." McMaster U, 4-5 November 1982.

_____. "The Paper People: A Television Play." *Canadian Drama/L'Art dramatique canadien* 9.1 (1983): 62-164.

_____. "The Tea Party, or How I was Nailed by Marian Engel, General Booth and Minn Williams Burge." *Room of One's Own* 9.2 (1984):35-40.

_____. *The Wars*. 1977. Markham, ON: Penguin, 1979.

Fitzgerald, Judith. "From *The Wars* to a Blind Cat on the Ark." *Globe and Mail* 2 July 1983: E3.

Fussell, Paul. *Abroad: British Literary Travelling Between the Wars*. 1980. Oxford: Oxford UP, 1982.

Galloway, David. *A Family Album*. London: Calder, 1978.

Geddes, Gary and Phyllis Bruce, eds. *Fifteen Canadian Poets*. Toronto: Oxford UP, 1970.

Gerson, Carole. "*Who Do You Think You Are?*: A Review/Interview with Alice Munro." *Room of One's Own* 4.4 (1979): 2-7.

Gervais, Mary. "An Ability to Strike the Right Chords." *Windsor Star* 16 Oct. 1982: A9.

Gibson, Graeme. *Eleven Canadian Novelists*. Toronto: Anansi,1972.

Gom, Leona. "Laurence and the Use of Memory." *Canadian Literature* 71 (1976): 48-58.

Gombrich, E.H. "Standards of Truth: The Arrested Image and the Moving Eye." *The Language of Images*. Ed. W.J.T. Mitchell. 1974. Chicago and London: U of Chicago P, 1980. 181-218.

Gutman, Judith Mara. *Lewis W. Hine and the American Social Conscience.* New York: Walker, 1967.

Hancock, Geoff. "An Interview with Alice Munro." *Canadian Fiction Magazine* 43 (1982): 74-114.

Hawthorne, Nathaniel. *The House of the Seven Gables.* New York: Bantam, 1981.

Heller, Joseph. *Catch-22.* New York: Dell, 1964.

Hemingway, Ernest. "Soldier's Home." *In Our Time.* 1925. New York: Scribner's, 1970.

Hill, Paul and Thomas Cooper, eds. *Dialogue with Photography.* New York: Farrar, 1979.

Hind-Smith, Joan. *Three Voices: The Lives of Margaret Laurence, Gabrielle Roy, Frederick Philip Grove.* Toronto: Clarke, Irwin,1975.

Hulcoop, John F. " 'Look! Listen! Mark my Words!': Paying Attention to Timothy Findley's Fictions." *Canadian Literature* 91 (1981):22-47.

_____. "The Will to Be." *Canadian Literature* 94 (1982): 117-122.

Irvine, Lorna. "Changing is the Word I Want." *Probable Fictions: Alice Munro's Narrative Acts.* Ed. Louis MacKendrick. Downsview: ECW, 1983. 99-111.

Isherwood, Christopher. "A Berlin Story." *The Berlin of Sally Bowles.* London: Hogarth, 1975.

Klovan, Peter. " 'Bright and Good': Findley's *The Wars.*" *Canadian Literature* 91 (1981): 58-69.

Kroetsch, Robert. "The Exploding Porcupine: Violence of Form in English-Canadian Fiction." *Open Letter* 5th ser. 4 (1983): 57-64.

Kröller, Eva-Marie. "The Exploding Frame: Uses of Photography in Timothy Findley's *The Wars.*" *Journal of Canadian Studies* 16. 3/4 (1981): 68-74.

Larkin, Philip. "Lines on a Young Lady's Photograph Album." *Twentieth-Century Poetry and Poetics.* Comp. Gary Geddes. Toronto: Oxford UP, 1973.

Laurence, Margaret. *A Bird in the House.* Toronto: McClelland, 1970.

_____. *The Diviners.* Toronto: McClelland, 1974.

_____. *The Fire-Dwellers.* Toronto: McClelland, 1969.

_____. *The Fire-Dwellers.* ts. McMaster U Special Collections, Hamilton, Ontario.

_____. "Gadgetry or Growing: Form and Voice in the Novel." Woodcock 80-89.

_____. *Heart of a Stranger.* Toronto: McClelland, 1976.

_____. *A Jest of God.* Toronto: McClelland, 1966.

_____. *A Jest of God.* ts. McMaster U Special Collections, Hamilton, Ontario.

_____. *The Prophet's Camel Bell.* Toronto: McClelland, 1963.

_____. "A Statement of Faith." Woodcock 56-60.

_____. *The Stone Angel.* Toronto: McClelland, 1964.

_____. "Time and the Narrative Voice." Woodcock 150-59.

_____. *The Tomorrow-Tamer*. 1963. Toronto: McClelland, 1970.

_____. *This Side Jordan*. 1960. London: Macmillan, 1961.

Lee, Dennis. *Savage Fields: An Essay in Literature and Cosmology*. Toronto: Anansi, 1977.

Lewinski, Jorge. *The Camera at War: A History of War Photography from 1848 to the Present Day*. London: Allen, 1978.

Lieberson, Jonathan. Rev. of *Diane Arbus: A Biography* by Patricia Bosworth. *New York Review of Books* 16 Aug. 1984: 9-12.

Macfarlane, David. "The Perfect Gesture." *Books in Canada*Mar. 1982: 5-8.

MacLulich, T.D. "Ondaatje's Mechanical Boy: Portrait of the Artist as Photographer." *Mosaic* 14. 2 (1981): 107-19.

McNeilly, Anne. "Happiness Depends on Viewpoint." *Kitchener-Waterloo Record* 17 Feb. 1979: 74.

MacSkimming, Roy. "The Good Jazz." *Canadian Literature* 73 (1977): 92-94.

Mallinson, Jean. "John Robert Colombo: Documentary Poet as Visionary." *Essays on Canadian Writing* 5 (1976): 67-70.

Manguel, Alberto. "Findley's People." *Books in Canada*, June-July 1984: 13-16.

Metcalf, John. "A Conversation with Alice Munro." *Journal of Canadian Fiction* 1.4 (1972): 54-62.

Moss, John. *A Reader's Guide to the Canadian Novel*. Toronto: McClelland, 1981.

_____. *Sex and Violence in the Canadian Novel: The Ancestral Present*. Toronto: McClelland, 1977.

Mundwiler, Leslie. *Michael Ondaatje: Word, Image, Imagination*. Vancouver: Talonbooks, 1984.

Munro, Alice. "The Colonel's Hash Resettled." *The Narrative Voice: Short Stories and Reflections by Canadian Authors*. Ed. John Metcalf. Toronto: McGraw, 1972. 181-83.

_____. *Dance of the Happy Shades*. Toronto: McGraw, 1968.

_____. *Lives of Girls and Women*. Toronto: McGraw, 1971.

_____. *The Moons of Jupiter*. Toronto: Macmillan, 1982.

_____. "An Open Letter." *Jubilee* 1 (1974): 5-7.

_____. *Something I've Been Meaning to Tell You: Thirteen Stories*. Toronto: McGraw, 1974.

_____. "What is Real?" *Making It New: Contemporary Canadian Stories*. Ed. John Metcalf. Toronto: Methuen, 1982. 223-26.

_____. *Who Do You Think You Are?: Stories*. Toronto: Macmillan, 1978.

_____. "Working for a Living." *Grand Street* 1.1 (1981): 9-37.

Murch, Kem. "Name: Alice Munro. Occupation: Writer." *Chatelaine* Aug. 1974: 42+.

New, William H. "Fiction." *Literary History of Canada: Canadian Literature in English*. Ed. Carl F. Klinck. Vol. 3. 2nd ed. Toronto: U of Toronto P, 1976. 3 vols.

_____. "The Other and I: Margaret Laurence's African Stories." *A Place to Stand On: Essays by and about Margaret Laurence*. Ed. George Woodcock. Edmonton: NeWest, 1983. 113-34.

Newhall, Beaumont. *The History of Photography: From 1839 to the Present Day*. 1939. 4th ed. New York: Museum of Modern Art, 1978.

Nodelman, Perry M. "The Collected Photographs of Billy the Kid." *Canadian Literature* 87 (1980): 68-78.

Ondaatje, Michael. *The Collected Works of Billy the Kid: Left-Handed Poems*. Toronto: Anansi, 1970.

_____. *Coming Through Slaughter*. Toronto: Anansi, 1976.

_____. *The Dainty Monsters*. Toronto: Coach House, 1974.

_____. *Leonard Cohen*. Toronto: McClelland, 1970.

_____. *Rat Jelly*. Toronto: Coach House, 1973.

_____. *Running in the Family*. Toronto: McClelland, 1982.

_____. *Secular Love*. Toronto: Coach House, 1984.

_____. *There's a Trick with a Knife I'm Learning to Do: Poems 1963-1978*. New York: Norton, 1979.

Porter, Katherine Anne. "Old Mortality." *Pale Horse, Pale Rider: Three Short Novels*. 1936. New York: Modern Library, 1939. 9-61.

Pound, Ezra. "Hugh Selwyn Mauberley." *Personae: The Collected Poems of Ezra Pound*. New York: New Directions, 1926.

Ricou, Laurie. " 'Obscured by Violence': Timothy Findley's *The Wars*." *Violence in the Canadian Novel Since 1960*. Eds. Virginia Harger-Grinling and Terry Goldie. St. John's: Memorial U, n.d. 125-37.

Rocard, Marcienne. "Margaret Laurence S'oriente-t-elle vers un roman audio-visuel? " *Etudes canadiennes*. 8 (1980): 113-20.

Rosenblum, Naomi. *A World History of Photography*. New York: Abbeville, 1984.

Rosengarten, H. J. "Innocence Confused." *Canadian Literature* 36 (1968): 77-80.

Scharf, Aaron. *Art and Photography*. 1968. Harmondsworth, Eng.: Penguin, 1983.

Scobie, Stephen. "*Coming Through Slaughter*: Fictional Magnets and Spider's Webbs." *Essays on Canadian Writing* 12 (1978): 5-22.

_____. "Two Authors in Search of a Character: bp Nichol and Michael Ondaatje." *Poets and Critics: Essays from* Canadian Literature *1966-1974*. Ed. George Woodcock. Toronto: Oxford UP, 1974. 225-46.

_____. "A Visit with Alice Munro." *Monday* 19 Nov. 1982: 12-13.

Sekula, Allan. "On the Invention of Photographic Meaning." *Thinking Photography*. Ed. Victor Burgin. London: Macmillan, 1982. 84-109.

Solecki, Sam. "An Interview with Michael Ondaatje." *Rune* 2(1975): 39-54.

_____. " 'The Making and Destroying': Michael Ondaatje's *Coming Through Slaughter* and Extremist Art." *Essays on Canadian Writing* 12 (1978): 24-47.

_____. "Michael Ondaatje." *Descant* 14. 42 (1983): 77-88.

Sontag, Susan. "Fascinating Fascism." *A Susan Sontag Reader*. New York: Farrar, 1982. 305-25.

_____. *On Photography*. 1973. New York: Delta Books, 1977.

Stevens, Mark. "Revival of Realism." *Newsweek* 7 June 1982: 64-70.

Stott, William. *Documentary Expression and Thirties America*. New York: Oxford UP, 1973.

Stouck, David. *Major Canadian Authors: A Critical Introduction*. Lincoln: U of Nebraska P, 1984.

Struthers, Tim. "Alice Munro and the American South." *Canadian Review of American Studies* 6.2 (1975): 196-204.

_____. "Munro's Latest Shows 'Astonishing' Maturity." Rev. of *Who Do You Think You Are? London Free Press* 8 Dec.1978: B5.

_____. "Reality and Ordering: The Growth of a Young Artist in *Lives of Girls and Women*." *Essays on Canadian Writing* 3 (1975): 32-46.

_____. "The Real Material: An Interview with Alice Munro." *Probable Fictions: Alice Munro's Narrative Acts*. Ed. Louis MacKendrick. Downsview, ON: ECW, 1983. 5-36.

Szarkowski, John, ed. *E.J. Bellocq: Storyville Portraits: Photographs from the New Orleans Red-Light District, Circa 1912*. New York: Museum of Modern Art, 1970.

Tagy, John. "The Currency of the Photograph." *Thinking Photography*. Ed. Victor Burgin. London: Macmillan, 1982. 110-41.

Taylor, Michael. Rev. of *The Wars* by Timothy Findley. *Fiddlehead* 118 (1978): 172-74.

Thomas, Clara. *The Manawaka World of Margaret Laurence*. Toronto: McClelland, 1976.

_____. *Margaret Laurence*. Toronto: McClelland, 1969.

Thomas, D.M. *The White Hotel*. Harmondsworth, Eng: Penguin, 1981.

Thompson, Eric. "Of Wars and Men." Rev. of *The Wars* by Timothy Findley, and other works. *Canadian Literature* 78 (1978): 99-101.

Watney, Simon. "Making Strange: The Shattered Image." *Thinking Photography*. Ed. Victor Burgin. London: Macmillan, 1982. 154-76.

Webster, Frank. *The New Photography: Responsibility in Visual Communication*. London: John Calder, 1980.

Welty, Eudora. *One Writer's Beginnings*. Cambridge: Harvard UP, 1984.

Wilson, Ann. "*Coming Through Slaughter*: Storyville Twice Told." *Descant* 14.42 (1983): 99-111.

Woodcock, George, ed. *A Place to Stand On: Essays by and about Margaret Laurence*. Edmonton: NeWest, 1983.

INDEX